Far From the

Green Fields of Erin

Ulster emigrants and their stories

David Hume

For Sandra, Rory, Christopher and Daniel

Farewell to the Green Fields of Erin,
farewell to the land I was born
farewell to Aul Wassagh, Ballyedward,
and the dear friends of sweet Magheramorne

James Barry's Farewell
William James Hume, 1921

6 5 4 3 2 1

© Dr David Hume
   and Colourpoint Books 2005

Designed by Colourpoint Books, Newtownards
Printed by ColourBooks Ltd

ISBN 1 904242 42 1

Colourpoint Books
Jubilee Business Park
21 Jubilee Road
NEWTOWNARDS
County Down
Northern Ireland
BT23 4YH
Tel: 028 9182 0505
Fax: 028 9182 1900
E-mail: info@colourpoint.co.uk
Web-site: www.colourpoint.co.uk

Dr David Hume was born in Carrickfergus, County Antrim, and was educated at Ballycarry Primary School, Larne High School and the University of Ulster. A journalist for 15 years with the *Larne Times* in County Antrim before taking up the post of Director of Services for the Grand Orange Lodge of Ireland in 2003, he is also actively involved in a number of community and voluntary bodies in his local area. David Hume has delivered history lectures to many groups across Northern Ireland as well as in the Republic of Ireland, Scotland, England and the United States, and is a regular columnist with *The Ulster Scot*, publication of the Ulster Scots Agency. He has an abiding interest in the subject of Ulster emigrants and has researched the subject over a number of years. Married with three sons, he is also an Honorary Citizen of Clover, South Carolina.

Unless otherwise credited, all photographs are by the author or taken from the author's collection.

Cover photographs:
Front: Atlantic sunset from Rossnowlagh, Co Donegal.
Norman Johnston

Rear, left: Centrepiece at the Andrew Jackson State Park on the boundaries of North and South Carolina is this impressive statue of the young Jackson on horseback. *Author*

Rear, right: GI bride Ruby Mewhirter and her husband Charles Rudzinski on their wedding day at Larne Methodist Church on 28 September 1944. *courtesy Ruby Rudzinski*

Contents

Song of the Antrim Harvester in Canada
by an American Exile, November 1923.[1]

My native land is Erin,
Above the wave appearing,
No place is more endearing
No matter where I roam.
Where boreal winds are blowing
Mid Arctic weather, snowing
Beside the warm fire glowing
I sit and dream of home.

When my dear mother blessed me
When leaving, and caress'd me,
Sad thoughts of home oppressed me,
I fondly feel them still;
when musing on the rambles
and all our youthful gambols,
in the glen among the brambles,
in the shadow of the hill.

And thro' the woods entangling
I hear our boyish wrangling
For the hazel nuts a-dangling
on the bough above the thorn;
And I jocund laugh resounding
where o'er the meadows bounding
the honeyed hive surrounding
On a dreamy summer morn

The reapers joyous singing
their sickles stoutly swinging,
the golden sheaves a-flinging,
And the rustle of the corn.
No southern sky is clearer,
no land to know is dearer,
And heaven itself seems nearer
When I think on Craiganorne.

The summer sky is brighter
the Autumn frosts are lighter
And winter snow falls whiter
Oh Ireland, mavrone!
Where the flowering gorse is growing,
I can hear the river flowing.
And the cattle gently lowing
By the well of Craiganorne.

There passed our childhood hours
In a wilderness of flowers,
In the green embroidered bowers
Of the Glen where I was born.

There sorrow never chased us,
but joys etheral graced us;
Dark misery never traced us,
Or grief could ever find;
We prayed the sunshine's pleasure
to gather it at leisure
And danced a happy measure
to the piping of the wind.

Where heaven is blue above her
I cannot cease to love her –
May guardian angels hover
Around my Mother Isle
And Thou, the Mighty Donor!
Bestow Thy gifts upon her,
And send her peace, and honour,
And light her with Thy smile.

---

[1]   *Belfast Weekly Telegraph*, author unknown, November 1923

Foreword
by The Lord Laird of Artigarvan

The Province of Ulster, on the island of Ireland, has, for many hundreds of years, been a cauldron of peoples of differing backgrounds and religions all trying to practice their ways of life and in some cases failing. Near to the Scottish coast and cut off from the rest of the island of Ireland by natural physical barriers, Ulster would bubble up and over-heat time and time again. New peoples being 'thrown into the melting pot' and others leaving.

It was from that human crossroads that decade after decade families, entire congregations and in some cases, populations of areas, left Ulster shores to find or make a new life. There must be a better way many thought – to express their desires for free thinking and thus freedom.

The social, moral and religious demands of the time, not to mention the undercurrent of strife and the need for back-breaking work, developed a particular type of people when exported.

Dr David Hume's outstanding insight into those who left these shores and made a new life mostly in the 'New World' is an important contribution for these under-recorded folk. Rightly, Dr Hume points to the part that very many Ulster Scots/Scotch Irish made in the creation and development of North America. Possibly no group of 400,000 people in this case moved from the borders of Scotland and England to Ulster in the 17th Century, have had such an impact on the modern world.

In recent years many like myself have been thrilled and delighted by the growing recognition of the Ulster Scots role around the world. New concepts in politics, underlining values in religion, new innovations in farming and new technology in manufacturing are all part of their legacy. An outward looking, freedom loving, independent minded people, their footprints can be found over vast continents and other locations.

While I, as an Ulster Scot, am keen to recognise that group's achievements around the world, I do know that others from differing backgrounds left our shores and contributed to developments in many areas. These worthy folk are also honoured by Dr Hume. Recognition for all is important and would be less than honest if not available.

What a place Ulster, was and is. What an impact on the 'New World'. How can we ever understand and acknowledge Ulster people's roles? Possibly never to its proper extent.
But whatever happens, David Hume's research, and as a result this book, is a vital step in understanding who we are and why.

The Lord Laird of Artigarvan
House of Lords
London

Acknowledgements

Research for this book has taken place over several years, and the finished product is not intended to be an exhaustive account of those many who emigrated from the north of Ireland from the 18th century onwards; indeed, such a task would be almost impossible. It is hoped, however, that it reflects the varied experiences of the many men, women and children who made journeys to other lands and new worlds.

I would acknowledge with gratitude the assistance of many in my research over several years. Several of those who were in correspondence with me have since passed away, and will not know how significant their assistance proved to be; they were carriers of a flame which will hopefully pass to others in their respective regions of the world where Ulsterfolk had settled.

My gratitude is duly expressed to all those who helped in any way in the research and preparation of this study, including those mentioned below, whose assistance and advice was particularly helpful:

The Barry family of Loch, Victoria, who still hold County Antrim in their hearts.

Roy F Blair, of Union County, South Carolina, for information on the John Blair Journal of 1796 and the Blair family in the USA.

Stanley C Brown of Tucson, Arizona, for details on Joseph McLernon, County Antrim cavalryman killed in the Indian Wars.

Carroll S Caldwell of Spartanburg, South Carolina, who lives on the soil farmed on the Reidville Road by his Ulster ancestors from the 18th century.

CC Caldwell and his late wife Harriet, who first introduced me to the Ulster heritage of their beloved Carolinas.

The late Hellene Carlisle, proudly Ulster-Scot historian of Nazareth Presbyterian Church, Spartanburg, South Carolina.

Kevin Donleavy, Ivy, Virginia, for information on John Neilson of Ballycarry, one of President Thomas Jefferson's personal friends.

David McCutcheon, Larne, for helpful information on Irish Freemasonry abroad.

Professor Bobby Gilmer Moss, historian and Ulster-Scot, for providing guided tours and many stories relating to Ulster-Scots patriots at the battles of Kings Mountain and Hanna's Cowpens, South Carolina.

James Murray, formerly of Glenarm, a modern day European emigrant to Sweden, for information on artist William Coulter of San Francisco.

Ron Murray, a modern emigrant to Wairarapa, New Zealand.

The late Richard Robinson of Las Vegas for memories of his earlier life in Larne and his new life in the United States..

Ruby Rudzinski (nee Mewhirter) of Baltimore, Maryland, USA, one of Ulster's GI brides, for sharing her wonderful memories of a fairytale romance that lasted over 50 years.

Peggy Sample, Dundas, Ontario, for information on the Semple family of Magheramorne and Ontario.

The late Roy Sproule of Ballycarry for information on his father-in-law William Calwell, an emigrant who returned from California.

Sam Thomas of the Historical Commission of York County, for archive information.

Marnie Thompson, Vancouver, for information on the Clarke brothers of Ontario East.

Colin Tweed, Milton, New Zealand, for information on Margaret McDowell of County Antrim and Lovell's Flat, New Zealand

David Verran, Local History Librarian, Auckland City Libraries, for information on the County Tyrone Entrican brothers.

Denis Whiteside of Brampton, Ontario, for sharing his story of emigration and a new life in Toronto in the 1940s and 1950s.

Dr Gerry Slater, Keeper of the Records, Public Record Office of Northern Ireland, for permission to use archive material.

Finally, my thanks go to Norman Johnston and Paul Savage at Colourpoint Books for turning the numerous A4 pages of my manuscript into the splendid volume you see before you.

Parts of the world that are forever Ulster

As a young boy I remember a visit to our farm one day from a tall man with a strange accent. Standing inside our barn looking towards the door which he framed, this man seemed incredibly tall. His name was Wilson Barry. In later years I would understand much more about Wilson Barry and his visit. He had a strange accent because he had been in Australia many years, and the reason for his visit that day was to in some sense come home, because as a young boy he had spent his last night in Northern Ireland at our farm, his parents and other siblings being offered beds in the neighbours farms prior to the Barry's departure for Melbourne and a new life in Victoria. Wilson's visit was lost in the mist of childhood somewhere, but in later years the importance of their Ulster roots to the Barry family in Australia would become very clear, as successive members of the family – and new generations – made that pilgrimage back from Victoria to the land that James and Susan Barry had left with their children in 1921.

My grandfather, who was something of an entertainer in the locality, wrote and performed songs and poems, and among his faded handwritten collection is one titled *James Barry's Farewell*. It was written as a tribute to his neighbour before he left for good. In the 1990s I received a package of material relating to the family in Australia from Heather Barry, one of the modern generations of the family and among the documents was a copy of *James Barry's Farewell*. The words of the song must have meant something very special for it to have been carried by James Barry on his journey and preserved by others when he reached his journey's end in a land far away from 'the dear friends of sweet Magheramorne'. We will return to the story of the Barrys in another chapter, but suffice to say that they help to illustrate how, despite emigration to a new life and new world, a sense of place remains strong for the land that was left behind. That sense of place may not occur with all emigrants, but it is nevertheless an understandable emotion for the generation directly involved; it's survival and progression through new generations must surely testify to its great strength.

I experienced something of this sense of emotional value attached to the concept of place when I visited the Waxhaw cemetery in Lancaster County, South Carolina. The cemetery there is bordered by mature trees on the north and east, and wandering through it and reading the gravestones makes it possible for one to believe they are somewhere thousands of miles away in Antrim, Down or Tyrone. The surnames on the gravestones provide the strong impression that this is a small part of the United States that is forever Ulster. Standing in the midst of that little graveyard, I felt a strange sense of affinity with the landscape around. Those buried there might have long gone, but the landscape was a connection with the past, and it was possible to imagine earlier times in the Waxhaws.

Just as the Barry family of Ballarat are not known in a wider sense, so too there are many buried at Waxhaw cemetery who have not been actors on the wider stage, but merely lived their lives in quiet and anonymity as far as the rest of the world is concerned. In front of the church a memorial stone informs visitors that the Waxhaw Presbyterian Church (which sits at the south-east corner of the cemetery) was organised by Ulster-Scots, or Scotch-Irish, in 1755. We learn from the memorial that Robert Miller was schoolteacher and minister there in 1758, while Rev William Richardson occupied the pulpit between 1759 and 1771. The church was used by the Americans during the Revolutionary War as a hospital. It was a log building back then, and no doubt burned quickly when King George's Redcoats set it ablaze.

Thomas McDow, whose stone is near the church, epitomises the link between exiled Ulster Presbyterian congregations and the Revolution. His gravestone tells us he was a Private in the South Carolina troops of the War, and also Ruling Elder of Waxhaw Church. He survived the war, passing away at the age of 70 years. Further to the north in the cemetery, we know much about County Antrim man William Blair by a reading of his gravestone. Born in County Antrim, we are told, he passed away in 1824 at 9 o'clock in the evening in the 66th year of his age; "When about 13 years old he came with his Father and family to this Country, where he resided till his death" we learn. Blair's large horizontal gravestone is completely carved with the story of a man who was:

> . . . a revolutionary patriot.
> And in the humble stations of private soldier and waggon master it is believed he contributed more essentially to the

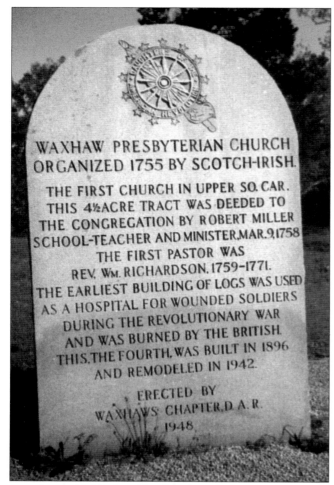

A marker outside Waxhaw Church outlines the history of of the church and congregation, one of those founded by Ulster Scots settlers in America in the 18th century. The original building was burnt down by troops during the Revolutionary War because it had been used as a hospital to nurse wounded Americans.

It is the mention of place that always strikes a chord when you view it on a gravestone thousands of miles from home. W James McCrey was born in County Antrim in 1870 and died in 1908, a later Ulster arrival into the garden of the Waxhaw. One wonders what network brought him there and whether the same network was responsible for the arrival of Andrew McMullan from Derrykeighan, County Antrim. His memorial stone informs us that he died in August 1825 at the age of 75 years, while his wife Sarah lies buried beside him and was from the parish of Loughgiel in County Antrim. William McMullan, whose stone is nearby, was also from Derrykeighan and died in 1881 at the age of 76.

What brought those 19th century Ulster settlers to the Waxhaws can not be gleaned from their stones. Walking through the little cemetery, bordered by tall trees on two sides and the road on the other, one finds other Ulster links: David Cousar, a native of County Armagh, who died in July 1807 at the age of 39, was one of a number of those of the same surname interred there. Other gravestones do not mention a place of origin. But then again, they do not have to. Apart from the Davie plot, commemorating a well-to-do family from England, most everyone else buried there came from

The gravestone of Mary Ann McCrey is one of several in the Waxhaw cemetery which mention locations in Northern Ireland.

establishment of American independence than many whose names are proudly emblazoned on the page of history. With his father's waggon he assisted in transporting the baggage of the American army for several months . . . He was also in the battles of the Hanging Rock, The Eutaw, Ratcliff's bridge, Stono and the Fish dam ford on broad river. In one of these battles (it is not recollected which) he received a slight wound: but so far from regarding it, either then or afterwards, when it was intimidated to him that he might avail himself of the bounty of his Country and draw a Pension (as many of his Camp associates had done) he declared that, if the small competence he then possessed failed him he was both willing and able to work for his living, and if it became necessary to fight for his country without a penny of pay.

the North of Ireland. There are a lot of Crawfords (who were related to the Jacksons), Montgomerys, Thompsons, Greers, Harpers, Fosters, Dunlaps, Cairns, Crocketts and others. One of the Crocketts, John, we are told from the gravestone, was born on a ship bound for Pennsylvania in 1730. The experience did him little harm; he lived to the age of 70 years and five months.

The Waxhaw settlement would be relatively anonymous, like many others dotted across the United States, Canada, Australia or elsewhere where Ulsterfolk have settled, but for the fact that it is linked to the seventh President of the United States, a figure still regarded in high esteem as a hero of the common man, founder of a modern political party (the Democratic Party) and a great general. Andrew Jackson might have started his legend by refusing to blacken a British officer's boot in the Waxhaw during the American Revolution, but his real claims to fame lay elsewhere. He was the hero of the Battle of New Orleans in 1815, when the Americans inflicted a fatal defeat on the finest army in Europe at the time and confirmed their independence from Great Britain. The story of the Battle of New Orleans has been immortalised over the years by Lonny Donegan, the Nitty Gritty Dirt Band, Johnny Cash and others, and with it the name of Andrew Jackson has been again brought to the fore. Jackson was also the hero of the common man, the first non-aristocrat to enter the White House. He was, to use a good Ulster term, rough and ready. An often contradictory character,[2] he proved a strong leader at a formative period in American history. In the town of Lancaster in South Carolina there is a wall mural of famous sons and daughters of the county and the portrait of Andrew Jackson forms the beginning of this 'wall of fame'. But out in the county, at Waxhaw cemetery, it is not Andrew who is chiefly commemorated (he left the area for Tennessee and is buried with his wife Rachel Donelson in the grounds of his home, the Hermitage, in Nashville). There are gravestones commemorating his father, Andrew Snr, who died just before his son was born, and his brothers Hugh and Robert, both of whom died during the American Revolution. But the most imposing memorial is a statue in honour of his mother, Elizabeth Hutchinson Jackson.

Elizabeth was among the women who took a stand during the Revolution against the Crown, and it was because she and Agnes Craighead and others had used the Waxhaw church as a hospital that it was burned. Elizabeth was a woman of outstanding strength and tenacity. When her sons were imprisoned for supporting the Patriot cause she rode across the country into North Carolina to plea for their release, something which she eventually managed to achieve. It was too late for one of them, Robert, unfortunately, as he died shortly afterwards, but she managed to nurse Andrew back to health before leaving for Charleston to tend to American prisoners. It was while on a prison ship in

The memorial at the Waxhaw cemetery to Elizabeth Hutchinson Jackson, mother of the seventh US President, Andrew Jackson. The memorial was erected by the Daughters of the American Revolution.

Charleston that Elizabeth caught smallpox, from which she subsequently died. She was buried there, and even the efforts of her son as President failed to have her grave properly located. Andrew was planning on returning her to the Waxhaw, but it was not to be.

The monument placed by the Waxhaw Chapter of the Daughters of the American Revolution is outstanding in more ways than one. They praise the County Antrim woman

One of the plaques on the memorial to Elizabeth Jackson details how the County Antrim woman died of smallpox while nursing wounded soldiers during the American Revolution.

West of this marker is the site of a massacre of Ulster-Scots settlers of the Long Canes district of South Carolina. The attack took place during the Cherokee War of 1759–61. Relationships between the Native Americans and the settlers were often tense, although some Indian tribes such as the Catawba co-existed peacefully with the new influx of Europeans coming into the country.

for her tenacity in overcoming all the problems which beset her family in the 'garden of the Waxhaws'. Close by are a series of revolutionary war gravestones, among them two – in front of her memorial – to Elizabeth's two sons Hugh and Robert. One died of smallpox, one from sheer exhaustion in the harsh summer sun of the Carolinas. A short distance away is a marker in honour of Andrew Jackson senior, placed many years later by the Catawba Chapter of the Daughters of the American Revolution. All these memorials help to underline one essential truth: by November 1781 none of the family which had crossed the Atlantic remained; only Andrew, born at the farm of his uncle James Crawford in the Waxhaws, survived.

The settlement in that part of Lancaster County was one of the two oldest in the upcountry region of South Carolina. Settlers in the Long Canes area in Abbeville country, received land grants just three years before those who came to Waxhaw. Long Canes was planted by the Calhoun family and also had Ulster-Scots families living there, on what was the frontier of the colonial settlement. At Long Cane a massacre by Cherokee Indians claimed the lives of some of the settlers. In Waxhaw, a refuge was offered to those moving north in panic. The two settlements had something important in common. Long Canes had Ulster families, and those who had settled at the Waxhaws had generally come directly in the 1750s from what were called the 'Irish' settlements of the southern Shenandoah Valley of Virginia. Kinsmen and women were spreading into the Carolinas, and their legacy still remains strong there today.

For there is more to this than history on cemetery gravestones, interesting though it is. The Waxhaw Presbyterian Church still holds services, and still maintains a congregation.

In the area around the surnames of the families underline that the Ulster-Scots have laid down lasting roots. It is a far cry from the journey south on a great waggon road by the Jacksons of Bonnybefore, Carrickfergus, in 1765. But at the Waxhaw you can almost imagine that the stillness is a sign of approval. Pioneers rest there, who handed the baton to others still running, and the Waxhaw is a fine example of an emigrant Ulster community laying roots and a legacy down elsewhere.[3]

As at the Waxhaw, where the little Ulster settlement provided prominent names among the many who lived nondescript lives, so too at Long Canes another major figure in American history emerges. John Caldwell Calhoun's origins are not difficult to gauge from his middle and surname, and indeed the land peopled by the Calhouns and their settlement apparently included the townships of Hillsborough, Belfast and Londonderry. John Caldwell Calhoun, the son of Patrick Calhoun, is known as the Champion of the Old South in American history, but his relationship with Jackson was somewhat stormy. Calhoun served under Jackson as vice-president, but the latter was notorious for demanding his own way to the point of bullying his opponents, a somewhat unsavoury childhood trait he never seemed to grow out of. One biographer, Robert V Remini, notes:

> There was something of the bully in Andrew Jackson, both as man and boy. Sometimes he feigned anger as an excuse to release a flood of expletives, thereby terrorising those around him . . . although it now seems clear that his temper was more often than not under his complete control and was displayed only for effect [4].

That another Ulsterman with a strong opinion would not see eye to eye with Jackson can hardly be surprising, stubbornness being as a common enough trait of those settlers of Scottish stock from the north-east of Ireland. Thus Calhoun and Jackson came to a parting of the ways in 1832, when the former resigned from the cabinet. As it transpired their disagreement, over the issue of 'Nullification' (whether each state had the ultimate right to secede from the Union, as Calhoun argued) was a forerunner of much deeper and greater events to come in the United States in the 1860s. In that dispute, those of Ulster stock were to be found on both sides, and the relationships between them were not always the most favourable; Stonewall Jackson and Ulysses Simpson Grant were two remarkable and adept generals, for example, both on opposite sides in the conflict.

That Ulster descendants were divided during the American Civil War shows how the bonds of their ancestors were no longer so strong in a new land and with new generations. In the American Revolution most, although not all, Ulster settlers were strongly on the side of the Revolutionary cause. But in the War Between the States the 'community' was equally divided. The only difference is probably that in the southern states, where communities were smaller and more tightly-knit, the effects were felt on a much greater scale and with longer-term consequences.

An historical marker details the birthplace of Ulster-Scots politician John Caldwell Calhoun, described as 'The Statesman of the Old South'. Sections of the Calhoun lands in South Carolina had names such as Belfast, Hillsborough and Londonderry.

More positive relationships between those of Ulster descent are only tantalisingly barely seen when we consider some facts in relation to the most prominent of all those of Ulster emigrant stock. Ulster provided many Presidents of the United States, a list which needs little rehearsing and which starts with Andrew Jackson and has continued into modern times, with both Presidents Clinton and Bush claiming Ulster links.

It is interesting to note the connections which existed among prominent figures of Ulster stock in their own generations, although it would be much too sweeping without detailed research to suggest this was anything other than a product of 'extended coincidence' in that the Ulster-Scots emphasis on education may have helped provide a high proportion of their population base in the political, legal, and educational elites in various areas and they naturally gravitated in the same circles. Whatever the reason it is impressive to think of some major figures in the highest corridors of power. Andrew Jackson had, as noted, John Caldwell Calhoun as his Vice President. He also appointed James Buchanan, a future President with links to County Donegal and County Antrim, as Minister to Russia. James K Polk, another Ulster-American President, would appoint him Secretary of State in his administration. Andrew Jackson was much admired by Andrew Johnson, known in Tennessee as 'the mechanic governor' because of his working class background. Johnson's family had emigrated from a cottage in the Raloo area outside Larne, and he was born in Raleigh, North Carolina. In his political life, he was a follower of both Andrew Jackson and James Knox Polk. Jackson, meanwhile, was also on friendly terms with General Sam Houston, first President of the short-lived independent Republic of Texas, and former Governor of Tennessee. Sam Houston's roots lay on Ballyboley Mountain near Ballyclare in County Antrim. The pair first knew each other through their military career, and had a high mutual respect; at Rachel Jackson's funeral at the Hermitage, it was Sam Houston who led the pallbearers. Houston was also friendly with the Polks of Mecklenberg County in North Carolina and at least one letter sent to the family is on display at the Polk Museum there. The Polks were descended from Robert Polk (or, more probably, Pollock) of Londonderry and the family also had Donegal roots. James Knox Polk was elected to the US House of Representatives in 1825 and was a close associate of Andrew Jackson, being elected Speaker of the House during his second term and not being noted for his impartiality.

Among the prominent political and military figures in the US Civil War was Ulysses Simpson Grant, a future President whose roots lay in County Tyrone. During Andrew Johnson's administration Grant was Secretary of War for a short time, and he would serve as President between 1869 and 1877. He was, in fact, one of the few of the Ulster-American Presidents to visit his ancestral homeland. While Grant was firmly on the Union side in the conflict, General Stonewall Jackson was on the Confederate side, and a Presbyterian elder, his roots laying in the Birches district of County Armagh. And the highest ranking figure with local links was the former vice-president John Cabel Breckinridge, who came from the borderline state of Kentucky, which sided with the Union although many of her sons fought for the Confederacy, one detail being nicknamed 'the Orphan Brigade' in allusion to the situation. Breckinridge would be the last Confederate Secretary of War. The networks which had been existing to some degree prior to the war seem to have been shattered by it, and the great base of the Ulster-Americans in the south was considerably damaged by the outcome. In the twentieth century, some instances of these links can be found in the USA – President Theodore Roosevelt, for example, appointed Judge Richard Campbell to high judicial office in his administration, and both men had routes in County Antrim – but Canada is probably more fertile a soil for such connections in the period, a vast 19th century migration having secured Ulster population bases for generations.

Not all emigrants or their descendants became as famous as Andrew Jackson, Woodrow Wilson, Ulysses Simpson Grant or others of that ilk, of course. But there is what the Tyrone folk-poet WF Marshall referred to as 'a roll of honour' of emigrants which is undoubtedly headed by the famous. These include political leaders such as William Massey and John Ballance, New Zealand prime ministers, Hugh Nelson, Governor General of British Columbia, writers such as Edgar Allan Poe and Mark Twain, military figures including General Henry Knox in the American Revolution and Generals McClellan, Burnside and others in the Civil War, newspaper figures such as Horace Greeley and John W. Crockett (son of David) in the United States and William John Geddis in New Zealand, inventors and innovators such as Cyrus McCormick of farm reaper fame and Robert Dalzell, inventor of the grain elevator. The list continues, including clergymen, pioneers, artists, businessmen, and many more, the most far travelled of them being Neil Armstrong, who in addition to being the first man to set foot on the surface of the moon was also of County Fermanagh stock, and Colonel James Irwin, another of those to land on the moon, and whose grandparents were from Pomeroy in County Tyrone.

Those who were not so famous are legion and far scattered. The *Belfast News Letter* informs us in the summer of 1828 of the death of Hugh Magill at the inappropriately named Lucky Valley near Kingston, Jamaica, after a few days illness. Magill was eldest son of Hugh Magill of Belfast.[5] There are many hundreds of thousands of others. The spread of these people often meant that contact was lost with their families at home. Old copies of the *Weekly Telegraph* newspaper carry poignant columns of those seeking lost relatives; the edition of 11 May 1901, for example, carries one of many such notices over the years in which relatives have clearly lost touch; William Gillen of Ballee, Ballymena, was anxious to hear of the whereabouts of his uncle James Gillen, who had left Ballygarvey, Ballymena, in 1853 and last been heard of in Henry County, Kentucky, when he was acting as manager of one of the railways. Often a lack of literacy contributed to this inability to maintain regular contact, in James Gillen's case it may have been economic difficulty or a move to another state or region of the USA. While absence may have made some hearts grow fonder for home, some others undoubtedly concentrated on their new abodes to the detriment of their past life.

In an old family album I have photographs which show members of a now forgotten family in a far-off land of their adoption. Some depict a timber house; others show a young man and young woman, posing for the camera. He is sitting, his dog beside him, she is standing near the roadside, possibly on the front lawn of their house. Family folklore is sketchy, to say the least, and relates how two sisters were among those who left for Canada, one possibly ending up in the United States or Argentina. They married and their surnames changed, and so they became lost through the years, their

The Ulysses Simpson Grant ancestral homestead near Ballygawley in County Tyrone. Grant rose to political prominence after being an outstanding Union general during the American Civil War. *by kind permission of Dungannon District Council.*

story disappeared into the great melting pot produced by emigration and the fading of the family links.

Not all such circumstances end in failure, however, for the correspondence of James Callwell to his long-lost cousin in Canada in 1847 shows that communications were sometimes started many years after people had lost touch. His cousin Mary Jane Callwell was living in Kingston, Ontario, when he resumed contact with her in April that year, his letter indicating that Mary's father Henry had written to his Carrickfergus cousins shortly after she was born to tell them "the colour of your hair and eyes". But tragedy had struck shortly afterwards when Henry died, and his wife had not written to them; "How heart rending it was and still is, to think that my uncle died far from his native land and from his friends who held him dear and that your mother has deemed us, his friends, as unworthy of her trouble in writing to inform us that he was then no more...." James laments in his letter to his cousin. Part of the reasoning may have included the fact that Mary's mother had found a new husband and had no wish to contact the family of her deceased partner. This had the consequence, as the letter points out, of Mary Callwell knowing nothing of her father's

relatives in Ireland. Re-establishing contact was a difficult affair; James Callwell's first letter was returned from Kingston after the intended recipient could not be found. The second letter, which is now deposited in the Public Record Office of Northern Ireland, was taken by an acquaintance named Thompson who was emigrating to Ontario.[6]

And the example of another family, the Samples, shows how coincidence can often play a part in retracing the family histories of some of those who have left these shores for opportunities elsewhere. William Semple was born at Carnduff near Larne in 1815 and died in the house which he built in Goulbourn township near Ottawa in 1899. He was a shoemaker by trade and he and wife Matilda McCullough left Ulster in the early 1840s, along with one child. William had eight children with his wife before she died and then remarried and had another with widow Elizabeth Ebert, his second wife, who had ten other children. With so many descendants down the line it might be expected that connections would have been maintained by at least some with the family connection in County Antrim. But it was not until 2002 that Peggy Sample of Dundas, Ontario, began to try and trace the ancestral trail. Determined to visit the land of her ancestors, just before she left Canada an uncle contacted her to tell her of some letters which had been locked away in a chest for years. The letters provided the crucial clues which the Canadian needed; already in touch with a family historian in Larne, she now had an actual townland from the letter – Carnduff – which proved beyond value. After over 130 years the family link with Northern Ireland was re-established and the Carnduff Semples were traced.

Peggy found the letters which had been provided to her poignant reading. They are letters that speak of a yearning for reunion of a scattered family. One, from James and Mary J Semple at Carnduff on 21 March 1883, has "Write soon" written at the top. James was the brother of the emigrant, William, and it is clear from his letters that he fears the correspondence may not have arrived safely, and that he longs for closer contact with his brother. They provide family news including the death of a sister, called Jinny:

> We are all very sorry to say your sister Jinny is dead after a short illness. She was only six days ill. She took ill one Saturday evening sitting at the fire and died on the following Thursday about six o'clock in the evening. They kept her till Saturday about eleven o'clock, the funeral took place on the 22nd August 1882, aged 79 years of age. [7]

In 1883 William's "ever loving niece" Mary Jane Semple was also writing to Canada, her letter underlining that letters had arrived from Ontario at Carnduff; "I wish you were not so far away that we could see each other sometimes", she states. The correspondence from Carnduff also contained photographs, we learn from references in the letters, while others in the locality were seeking information about their own relatives through the Semples; details were being sought about Robert Girvin, as "his brother is always asking" one letter states.

The Semples would work hard in their new land, and William Semple would use his trade as a shoemaker to augment his income from farming. The land was rocky and one section of it was referred to by the family as 'the drownded lands' (a good Ulster term for the swampy land on part of the farm). In time the family home would be rebuilt of brick and the family would become prominent and prosper. Among the family members was Robert Nichol, who was Reeve of the Township (equivalent to a Mayor) as well as a prominent Orangeman, the family playing a part in Orange Day parades in Ottawa until the 1930s.

Sometimes coincidence can play an amazing part in the quest for lost emigrants. Many years ago two American ladies visited Ballycarry, County Antrim, in search of the gravestone of their ancestor, Rev Edward Brice, who was the first Presbyterian minister in Ireland and quite a major figure in his own right. Having met them, correspondence continued for several years with Janet Brice Hardin, who provided much material about the Ballymena branch of the Brice family which had settled in Fairfield County, South

An emigrant's homestead in Alberta, Canada; Ulster emigrants found that, unlike at home, houses were constructed of wood rather than brick.   *Author's collection*

Carolina. On one occasion they sent a photograph from one of the family homes still standing from the 18th century in the county. Years later, while being hosted in Clover, South Carolina, a party from Northern Ireland were taken to the plantation home recently purchased by one of the ladies in the town. This was located in Fairfield County and its name was Albion. This graceful white timbered Plantation house was surrounded by trees and a garden, and on the top story was a veranda from which it was possible to survey the grounds below. It appeared quintessentially southern Plantation, and was beautifully furnished inside. Among the furnishings in the entrance hall is an old framed map showing the area in the 18th century, and close examination reveals the names of the Ulster families who had settled the creeks nearby; the Douglasses and Brices prominent among them. There is no longer a house at Dumpers Creek, where John Brice and Mary Gardner had made their home, but on the old map it is possible to trace John and his brother William and other family members. Just beside the framed map was a painting of a plantation house. It was so similar to that photographed years before by Janet Brice Hardin that I almost suffered shock. Although almost completely sure that this was the house Janet and her sister had visited, I waited until I had returned to Northern Ireland before searching out the original and accompanying letter – and realised beyond all doubt that, amazingly, I had inadvertently been in the home of the Douglass cousins of the Brices, and that Ballymena accents had once echoed around that house. Having never given consideration to the prospect of visiting the Douglass Plantation, and, indeed, having almost forgotten about it at that time, it was amazing that I had ended up there anyway. Coincidence can bring about some unexpected circumstances.

Robert Sample, who was the descendant of County Antrim emigrants to Goulbourn township in Ontario and had a long career in local politics in the area.

Photo supplied by Peggy Sample, Ontario, his great-granddaughter.

The Douglas house in Fairfield County, South Carolina, was built by a Ballymena family who emigrated to the area in the 18th century. The family were connected to the Brice family, Rev Edward Brice being the first Presbyterian minister in Ireland.

2   See, for example, Robert V Remini, Andrew Jackson, in three volumes, New York, 1998
3   Louis Pettus, The Waxhaws, Rock Hill, South Carolina, 1993
4   See Remini, Andrew Jackson, Volume One, op cit, p7
5   *Belfast News Letter*, 20 June 1828
6   Letter of James Callwell, Ballyhill, County Antrim, to his cousin in Kingston, Ontario, held in the Public Record Office of Northern Ireland, document T3614
7   Semple family correspondence, provided by Peggy Sample, Dundas, Ontario

Why and where they went

Emigration is a fascinating thing, perhaps because it is mostly about people removing themselves from one set of circumstances and placing themselves in another. Why did someone want to emigrate? Why did they go where they did? Were they fearful during their voyage at sea? Did things work out well for them or not? There are a hundred questions for each emigration. When one visits the sites which were settled by some of the earlier emigrants from our shores, it produces an unusual sense of time and place. Sometimes that sense was heightened by the fact that those involved choose to retain names from their homeland, as was the case at New Londonderry in New Hampshire, or Londonderry and Derry townships in Dauphin County, Pennsylvania. Unlike more individual emigration in the 20th century, such settlements often involved people who had travelled as a community. In 1772, for example, Rev William Martin took five shiploads of Ulster emigrants from ports such as Newry, Larne and Belfast, across the Atlantic to Charles Town, South Carolina. Their community was not only geographical, but also spiritual, for they were Covenanting Presbyterians, mainly from North Antrim, and their friends and relatives. The land grants awarded those from this group show a spread of locations across the Piedmont region of South Carolina, at places such as Fishing Creek, Laurens, Craven County, Fairfield County, Newberry, Waxhaw, Cedar Creek, Black Creek and many other locations[8], and they were in fact the ancestors of many of the Piedmont's Ulster-Scots community into more recent times.

In 1718 the first mass migration from Ulster had taken Rev James McGregor and five ships carrying around 900 emigrants from Aghadowey, Coleraine and Macosquin to New Hampshire, where they would form New Londonderry. The oldest man on the journey was the somewhat inappropriately named John Young, who was in his 90s, proving that age was no barrier to journeying and finding a new life with ones kith and kin. Often family or community networks were set in place which could be utilised to being others in a second and maybe third wave of emigration, as was alluded to by Thomas Wright, of Plumstead, Pennsylvania, in a letter to Thomas Greer of Dungannon, County Tyrone; "dear kind Friend I might just mention, by

The Ulster American Memorial in Larne's Curran Park commemorates over a quarter of a million people who emigrated from Ulster to America from 1717 onwards. One of the first emigrant ships, the Friend's Goodwill, sailed from the County Antrim port in May 1717, bound for Boston.

way of gratitude, if any of thy relations ever comes to this country and in my power to befriend them, all I can do shall be done as for my own family . . ." [9]

Neither was there any doubt, in the case of America, as Wright had stated, of the economic opportunities; "I seem to increase in worldly substance, ever since my last arrival, and Providence smiles on me in all my undertakings . . ." [10]

An advert from the *Weekly Telegraph* in 1906 announces reduced fares for those interested in emigrating to 'The settler's ideal home'. New Zealand became the home to many Ulster families.

William Faris, writing to his brother in Islandmagee, County Antrim, in 1800 from Turkey Creek, York, South Carolina, informed him that "he would rather be an indentured servant in this country than a cottier in Ireland," since conditions were so much better.[11]

When Ulster settlers were encouraged to establish a new settlement on his lands in Kati-Kati, New Zealand, in the 1870s, George Vesey Stewart of Ballygawley, County Tyrone, had the good sense to invite several of the new settlers to write accounts of their first year for the benefit of prospective settlers back in Ulster, the result being highly a favourable one, with comments on the wonderful climate, excellent new homes and highly productive soil. Some even attributed the New Zealand climate to alleviating bronchial complaints suffered by their children.[12]

For many who undertook voyages, however, a severe and uncertain time awaited, and it was not an experience that they wished to repeat. Samuel McCulloch, writing to his father in Carrickfergus in September 1774, detailed how he had lost his two daughters on the voyage: "...the two girls, to our great grief, both died in one hour. This was the greatest trouble I ever felt, to see our two fine girls thrown into the ocean after they had been seven weeks on board and were on the coast. Our mate died, and several more men and women and about 12 children. We had a great fever on board; men lay raving through all the berths. I never lay down that night, but I was afraid that some of us would have it before the morning. Our children died of a short illness and not of the fever."[13] This was not an uncommon occurrence, and it was sometimes physically compensated for by emigrant's naming children born in the new land after those who had failed to reach the promised shore.[14]

The emigrant abroad Family/Community Networks

Where emigrants settled, we often find family and community networks being established. In the case of Timber Ridge and Rockbridge County in Virginia, for example, we can identify the presence of Lyle, McDowell and Houston families among the settlers in the pre-Revolutionary period; these families were from the Gleno/Raloo/Ballyboley area of County Antrim.

The Magills, Beatties, Russells, Thompsons, and others from County Antrim settled at Beaver Creek, South Carolina, in the pre-Revolutionary period and would continue to welcome Beatties and Magills crossing the Atlantic into the 1800s. Prominent among the early Magills, for example, were James Boyd Magill and his wife Esther Rodgers, who came to the United States in 1823 and settled at Fishing Creek, Chester District, where they lived out their lives. Their son, James R Magill, was a prominent figure in the district and a member of the South Carolina House of Representatives and Senate.[15] In the Ballarat area of Australia we find not only Barrys from Magheramorne, County Antrim, but also Hunters from Ballycarry and Alexanders from Larne, and there is at least some evidence of connection between the settlement pattern and the families already there.[16]

Even those travelling in the United States (and probably elsewhere) knew of exiles in the area or would come across them in their travels; this is certainly the case with a Larne man named James Houston, who toured America from New Orleans north into Canada in 1836. In his letters home to his mother he details that while in New Orleans "I have been in a man's shop by the name of McCracken from Larne, it is in one of the best streets." In a subsequent letter from Madison, Indiana, he relates:

> I am quite comfortable in Mr McClean's. He is a native of Newry who was deeply engaged in the (1798) rebellion and had to leave Ireland then. He is not in any business nor farms any land but his houses in town let for near 4,000 dollars a year and he is still building more which are taken up as soon as furnished. His son with whom I made the acquaintance in New Orleans is in business very extensively but entirely in the wholesale way.

Houston detailed that he was planning to call for a few days with another Larne man, Agnew Farrel, who lived at Niagara Falls.[17]

For Protestant emigrants, two organisations in particular were important because of their presence in the new lands; the Orange Order and the Masonic Order. Members of Orange

Members of Canadian Loyal Orange Lodge 2710 display ornate sashes as they gather for this photograph taken many years ago. The symbols of the Bible and the Union Flag were important to Canadians and helped to cement the role of Orangeism in the Dominion. In turn, Orange lodges provided a social cement for new emigrants.

Lodges who were emigrating received a 'Travelling Certificate' verifying that they were in good standing. They would be encouraged and would feel inclined, to present this certificate and join an Orange lodge in Australia, Canada, New Zealand, the northern United States or other countries such as South Africa where lodges sat. This fraternal networking requires more research, but some such as Bruce Elliott have detailed how Orangeism helped establish classless networks for emigrants in Montreal:

> Though business associations, family relationships, and chains of godparenthood convey the impression of two distinct class-based groups of Tipperary Protestants in the city, the members of these two social levels shared common residential and migration patterns and were united by their common interest in the Orange Order.[18]

Given that in 1900 in Canada one in three male Protestants was an Orangeman, the networking role was obviously of high significance. This was repeated elsewhere, although with lesser numbers involved than in Canada.

A second influential fraternal body was the Masonic Order, which was universal and open to those of all religions, although in the Irish context it would probably be fair to say that by the 19th and 20th centuries it was predominantly Protestant. Freemasons could be assured of a welcome at a lodge in their chosen new homeland, and many came to play a prominent role. Belfastman James Taylor, for example, returned to visit his homeland in 1931 as Provincial Grand Master of the newly formed Masonic Province of Rhodesia. The *Belfast Weekly Telegraph* reported his return and detailed how he had joined the Masonic Order in 1901 in Belfast (Ulidia Lodge) and then helped to form a new lodge in Pietermaritzburg, capital of Natal, in 1910 (Ulidia Lodge). He later formed and became WM of St Patrick Lodge in Salisbury, Rhodesia, in 1921. Interestingly, Taylor's link with home remained in his new home in Salisbury where he and his wife lived at 'Knockbreda Park'.[19]

In Kansas City, Missouri, the East Gate Masonic lodge made a special presentation to Larne man Matthew Howard Orr in 1958. Orr, who was 73 years old, had been editor of the *North East News* in Kansas City before his retirement, but it was his 50 year service with the Masonic Order that was the occasion for the presentation. He had settled in Kansas City 30 years before, but obviously maintained associations

The Masonic section of a cemetery in South Carolina; many Ulster male emigrants belonged to the Freemasons.

that had started in 1905 in Strabane and continued when he affiliated to the East Gate lodge in the 1920s. Masonic links proved highly significant for many emigrants, among them Samuel Smiley Adrain, a member of lodges in Dublin and Larne, who emigrated to the United States in 1859. Unlike many other Masons, however, Adrain found that membership of the lodge at Orwicksburg, where he had originally settled, was difficult in view of the fact that the area was German in population and the lodge there 'worked' in the vernacular, which he could not understand. Moving to Meadville further west, he found himself at home in town and lodge, a contemporary account in the *Larne Monthly Visitor* from 1859 informs us.[20]

Church and Faith

Most emigrants, whatever their religion, were united by possession of a religious belief, and in no case was the strength of faith displayed than in Quebec in Canada, where a number of Canadian Catholic priests died of fever while ministering to large and doubtless despairing parishioners who had arrived on coffin ships from Ireland, seeking to flee the famine. Thousands died on Grosse Island, 50 kilometres

from Quebec City, while a monument today commemorates the clergy who gave their lives. An earlier memorial reminds the visitor of the mortal remains of 5424 persons at Telegraph Hill, "who flying from Pestilence and Famine in Ireland in the year 1847 found in America but a grave."[21] As one journalist of Irish descent pointed out, Grosse Ile "without ever seeking the honor, became the largest Irish Famine grave site in the world".[22] For many of those who sought a new life in the famine years, the spectre of fever would end their dreams. The courage of the Roman Catholic priests who ministered to the new arrivals at Grosse Ile is something of a re-run of the story of the Good Samaritan and an underlining of the strength a common faith held in new lands.

Faith and Fatherland were two strong pulls that often ensured that emigrants mixed and settled among their own countrymen when they could, and at least joined the church of their upbringing when they got to the new land. Thus it was that settlers from Ulster living in New Ulster, New Zealand, sent back a request to the Presbyterian General Assembly in 1853 asking for a minister, and received the assurance that Rev Mr John Mackey, minister of Fahan in County Donegal, would be appointed to them the following

Beaver Creek Presbyterian Church, South Carolina, was founded by a group of County Antrim emigrants led by the Russell family. The church remains an active congregation.   *courtesy Andee Steen, Stoneboro, South Carolina*

spring. Many churches in the American colonies owed their origins to the arrival of settlers from the North of Ireland, among them Middle Spring Presbyterian congregation in Pennsylvania, whose historian could refer to an "inborn Scotch-Irish Presbyterianism of the community".[23] The early elders of the congregation included men with familiar surnames such as Reynolds, McKee, Killough, Findlay, Herron, Mateer, and Anderson, while among those who became ministers from within the congregation in the century from its formation in 1738 were Thomas Orr, Stephen Wilson Pomeroy, John J Pomeroy, Alexander Kelso, John Wherry, Joseph Trimble, Joseph B McKee, and Francis Herron. Rev William Linn was the first son of the church to enter the ministry, being ordained around 1775, and was the oldest son of William Linn, a ruling elder of the church.[24]

The first three ministers at Middle Spring had come from Ulster, including Rev Thomas Craighead, born in Scotland, but who emigrated from Londonderry after living around ten years in the North of Ireland. He was followed by Rev John Blair, who had studied under William Tennent at his famous Log College at Neshaminy, Pennsylvania, and Rev Robert Cooper who was born around 1732 and came to Lancaster County, Pennsylvania, with his widowed mother and two sisters. The fourth of the early clergy was Rev John Moody, whose father Robert was a native of County Londonderry, who had emigrated to Cumberland County in Pennsylvania around 1773 and later settled with his wife Mary Hutchinson and family in Dauphin County, another area of strong Ulster settlement in Pennsylvania.[25]

Identifying the emigrants from official returns

It is, as Donald Harman Akenson points out, difficult to identity the numbers or the individual details of emigration, and true to say that by the times governments were concerning themselves enough the damage had been done.[26] There are various sources which give us information, however. Ships lists are one of these avenues; an 1804 Belfast list for the brig *Lady Washington*, bound for Charleston, South Carolina, in August details, for example, that among those on board were four Larne emigrants – John Sloan (22), a farmer from Glynn, John Crawford (25), a farmer from Mounthill and his wife Janet (22), and Alexander Aston (25), also from Mounthill and also a farmer. Another Mounthill couple, Thomas and Elizabeth Gordon appear on the list for the brig *Mary*, leaving Belfast for the Carolinas in September 1805.[27]

Similarly census and other statistical information can provide some details of interest to us, one example being information gleaned from Laurens County in South Carolina and the petitions for naturalization. These show many applying with details that there were natives of Ireland (and in this geographical context that means generally the north), but certain individuals identifying themselves also from particular counties. Alexander Stuart petitioned for naturalization in 1806, for example, stating himself to be a native of County Antrim who had lived in the United States for over ten years. His application is also of interest because of the names of those certifying as to his character; William Caldwell, Jno Simpson, William Dunlap, George Bowie, William Nibbs and JW McKeebin.[28] Anthony McFaul was a County Antrim man in his twenties and had came to America in 1811, while

FIRST SPRING SHIP
FOR PHILADELPHIA,
The fine new coppered & copper-fastened Ship
FRANCIS PEABODY,
To Sail about the 10th of MARCH.

This superior Ship has most comfortable accommodations
for Passengers, being very high and roomy between decks,
and her Berths will be fitted up in the most commodious
manner. As she will be the first vessel for that Port, and
much encouragement is held out to Emigrants for the United
States, those who are desirous of proceeding, should at once
secure Berths, as she will have quick despatch.

All necessary supplies for the voyage will be put on board,
and Passengers may rely on the Captain paying every attention to their comfort.

For Freight or Passage, apply to G. & T. M'TEAR, or
THOs. G. FOLINGSBY,
Hanover Quay.

Belfast, 7th Feb. 1829. (700

An advertisement from the *Belfast News Letter* of February 1829 outlining the first vessel to the port of Philadelphia and offering "much encouragement" to would-be emigrants to the United States.

John Cannon was from County Donegal, William Milligan from Antrim, John Ranson and John Ross from Monaghan, and Thomas Kirkpatrick was from Londonderry. His application tells us that he sailed from Belfast to Charleston in 1818. Others give interesting detail, such as the application by Andrew Matthews of the city of Londonderry, and we are informed that he arrived in Baltimore, Maryland, in September 1818 and the following year moved to Columbia in South Carolina. Andrew Kennedy was aged 41 years and had come from County Antrim, with his wife Ann Kennedy, aged 40. They had three children; Cunningham Moore Kennedy, who was 17 years old and had been born in County Antrim, Isabella, aged 14, who was born in County Meath, and John, aged 13, who was born in Meath as well. The family emigrated from Belfast in October 1823 and sailed to Charleston.[29]

The 1850 Federal Census for York District of South Carolina is still showing a number of citizens who say that they were born in Ireland, around 70 to 80 years after the bulk of the emigration from Ulster ports into the Carolinas and granting of land grants to emigrant families from the north of Ireland. Given the propensity for largely Presbyterian Ulster settlement into the area, and the surnames involved, it is possible to speculate that, as was the case at Beaver Creek elsewhere in the state, networks operated for emigration long after the turn of the 18th century.

Among those who list Ireland as their place of birth in the census are William Love, a 50 year-old labourer, David McElwain (69), Charles McElwain (67), whose household included Margaret (62, and presumably his wife), Leticia (22) and Margaret (21), Matilda Gettys (26), who was married to

EMIGRATION.
LARNE AGENCY.

Cheap Tickets to America
BY THE
ALLAN LINE ROYAL MAIL STEAMERS
From Derry Every Week.

EMIGRANTS CARRIED AT MUCH RE-
DUCED RAILWAY FARES to Derry
from the leading Stations. Full information,
Sailing Bills, and Pamphlets free on application
to the undersigned.

Passengers Booked at the Cheapest Fares to
the Australian Colonies, New Zealand, India,
China, The Cape, Buenos Ayres, Monte Video,
and all parts of the World, by the Orient Line,
Shaw Savill, New Zealand, Aberdeen, P. and
O., Anglo-Australian, Castle Line, Queensland,
German Line, and others.

Intending Emigrants will save money and
much trouble by consulting the

AUTHORISED AGENT:
JAMES BOYD,
Stationer, Larne.

9-2-89

An 1889 advert from the *Larne Reporter* offering "Cheap Tickets to America" as well as many other locations including New Zealand and Australia, Buenos Aires and India.

Ebenezer Gettys, born in Lancaster County, Pennsylvania, and had a two years old son, Thomas, and a baby daughter, Mary. Thomas and Mary Boyd, who were in their fifties, had both been born in Ireland, but their son John (22) had been born in Chester district, South Carolina, and 17 year-old daughter Ann was born in Fairfield County.[30] One trend which appears apparent enough is that, while in the

18th century emigrations, families moved en masse, in the 1850 census it would appear to be the case that while parents were born, and possibly married, in their native land, most children were being born in South Carolina; of the seven children of William and Mary Smith, for example, all but two had been born in the United States, these being aged 17 years and 15 years, while in many other cases all the children of the family were American-born.

Family histories

The importance of family history in preserving the story of the emigrants and their journey cannot be understated. Some families will retain items or papers relating to the homeland of those who emigrated, others will have anecdotes. The family histories attached to many provide some clues as to their origins. The historian of Greenwood County in South Carolina notes, for example, that, according to family tradition, the first of the McCaslan family to arrive from County Tyrone into America were Margaret, a widow, and her son Robert and daughter Mary. They arrived in Philadelphia, possibly soon after the American Revolution. Family tradition can often be a little sketchy, however, and there is some confusion as a family Bible records the marriage of Mary McCaslan to Moses Taggart in Ireland in 1790, adding that they landed in Charleston, South Carolina, in 1791. Perhaps the truth might be that the Taggarts arrived at one port, the McCaslan mother and son at another, but history has made it difficult to tell what is the correct version.[31] We do know, however, that Robert McCasland was a prominent member of Hopewell Presbyterian Church, that he became manager on the plantation of John Calhoun and died at the age of 82, being interred in the Long Cane Cemetery, in an area which once bore the township names Londonderry, Hillsborough and Belfast.

There are many other families, particularly in the United States, who had some knowledge – but not as much as they would like – of their ancestors who first crossed the ocean. This is also the case with other parts of the world such as Australia, New Zealand and Canada. New Zealander Colin Tweed is among the many thousands who have come back to Northern Ireland in search of their roots. His ancestor was Margaret McDowell from Magheramorne, who sailed for New Zealand in 1869 at the age of 17 years, accompanied by her sister and brother-in-law. The latter was named Glasgow Logan and he was a surveyor who had obtained 400 acres of bush at Owaka. Sixteen weeks after setting sail, the Antrim emigrants arrived at Dunedin on December 23, 1869, a voyage which would be followed by another ten day journey in stormy seas. At a place called Dutton's Sawmill, they spent their first weeks in New Zealand in a converted barn. Margaret McDowell would meet and marry Andrew Tweed of nearby Lovell's Flat and the union would see eight offspring. Margaret survived her husband, who died in 1910 at the age of 87, and passed away on June 6, 1944, aged 90 years. Colin Tweed's search for his Ulster roots have brought him from New Zealand twice, but as many seeking their family roots have found, it can often be difficult to tie up the ends when the threads have been broken over the years. One tangible reminder can still be found of Margaret McDowell and Andrew Tweed at Lovell's Flat – their old farm is sited on Tweed Road.[32]

John Caldwell, a native of Raloo, County Antrim, was among the 18th century emigrants to the Carolinas in the United States who also left something of a legacy[33]. John arrived in Spartanburg County, South Carolina, in 1766 or 1767 with his wife Mary and son William. When the American Revolution broke out, William was 16 or 17 years old and he took an active part on the American side, joining the Spartan Regiment of Colonel John Thomas. Among the battles the Raloo exile fought in was the Battle of Cowpens, at which the County Londonderry commander General Daniel Morgan was victorious over the British forces. After the war William Caldwell settled down to farm. Some years ago the original log house which the Caldwells built was discovered "inside" a later structure and has been relocated at the Nazareth Presbyterian Church, where it will be used for youth groups. The Caldwells gave some of their land for the Presbyterians of Wellford and Moore settlements to build the Nazareth Church, and their descendants remain in the area today.

Public notices in newspapers

The *Belfast News Letter* of 1869 conveyed the sad tidings that Henry Reid, the eldest son of John Reid of Granshaw, Bangor, had died at the age of 25 years of sunstroke in Cincinnati, Ohio.[34] Behind the simple insertion in the newspaper's public notices section, lies a much greater story,

Margaret McDowell from Magheramorne, County Antrim, who sailed for New Zealand at the age of 17 years along with her sister and brother-in-law. Married to Andrew Tweed of Lovell's Flat, New Zealand, she died in 1944 at the age of 90 years.

courtesy Colin Tweed, New Zealand.

no doubt. But the Births, Deaths and Marriages of papers provincial and local at least record the connections between homeland and land of adoption. The same edition of the *News Letter* carries the death notice of another Ulster exile, Cecilia Knox, wife of William James Knox, at the Rapids, Montreal in Canada. Marriage notices placed at home newspapers included those of George Wallace of Holywood, County Down, who was married to Annie Edmonds of Wellington, New Zealand, in March 1874 in the latter city,[35] while in 1909 a birth notice in a local newspaper informs us that the wife of Samuel Brennan, formerly of Ballygally, County Antrim, had given birth to a son in Transvaal. Brennan was, we also learn, employed in the Premier Mine there.[36] There must literally be thousands of such references over the years.

Sometimes the family historian or researcher can be fortunate in that much more than a mere notice appears. Such is the case with the death of John Dempsey, a 91 year-old native of Cairncastle, County Antrim, who died at Stratford, Ontario, in 1906. The account is highly detailed in outlining to us that Dempsey emigrated with his two brothers Hugh and Daniel in 1844 and settled in Stratford when it was a hamlet of just 17 families. A devoted member of the Episcopal Church, he helped erect the church building, and in 1846 married Mary Wilson, eldest daughter of Hugh Wilson of Downie township, taking his young bride to her new home in a wooden sleigh drawn by a yoke of oxen. *The Stratford Herald* was aware of the roots of many who had settled the area, referring to "those hardy old pioneers who came from the North of Ireland" and detailing some of them – the Nelsons, Robbs, Monteiths, Hessons, Wilsons, Boyds, Dunbars, Dempseys and Rankins. Such an article provides not only interesting detail about the individual but also information about his family and also the area in which he settled. Settlement was not necessarily a permanent thing, however, and some of the emigrants would appear to have been restless people. Robert Patterson, for example, a native of Clonmain, County Armagh, served for a time in the police force in Cheshire and then returned home to carry on farming pursuits. In 1927 he emigrated to New Zealand, living for a year in Palmerston North and then Tauranga, where he died at the age of 70 in 1936, being survived by his wife, three sons and five daughters.[37] Mary Gingles, who died in Illinois in 1949 was a native of Kilwaughter, County Antrim, and had emigrated to New Zealand to live with one of her two daughters in 1933. It was while visiting a second daughter in Illinois that she was taken ill and passed away. An obituary in the *Larne Times* in April 1949 noted that she was survived by seven daughters and two sons, both of whom lived in New Zealand. Her only surviving brother lived at Ballygowan, Ballynure, County Antrim.[38] Mary Gingles represents the example of many families who became somewhat scattered across the world through the process of emigration. But not all, of course, went so far. Although it

is without the scope of this volume, many thousands made new lives for themselves in Great Britain, where they found employment in mills and shipyards, and as agricultural labourers among other occupations; an example of an area of settlement is Kintyre, which, for generations, provided an area for close linkage between Scotland and Antrim. Research on Kintyre immigrant families in the Campbeltown area in the 19th century shows a high level of Antrim McMillans among the new arrivals, along with other surnames such as Anderson, Black, Dempsey, Dillon, Hamilton, Lamont, Laverty, McCormick, McIntyre and others. While Patrick McGill, a tailor, who was born in 1801, seems to have fared well for himself and his family, others were further down the social scale, with occupations such as fishermen, quarrymen, and farm workers and a number are reported to have died in Campbeltown poorhouse. Isabella McCurdie or Curdie, a farm worker, was born in 1788 and died in the poorhouse; although one might hope that three offspring who emigrated to America fared better.[39] The truth is probably that emigrants, wherever they went, had mixed fortunes.

Their legacy

The larger proportion of emigrants did not become famous as had Hugh Nelson, Lieutenant Governor of British Columbia between 1887–1892 and the son of Robert Nelson of Drumalis Terrace, Larne. But many did achieve status in their new homes and settlements, surrounded in many cases by others from this part of the world. When the prime minister of Northern Ireland, Sir James Craig and his wife, visited New Zealand in 1930 they were greeted in Auckland by 500 residents, all of Ulster stock, and oversaw the inauguration of an Ulster Society, membership being based on birth within the nine counties of the historic province of Ulster.[40]

Many of the emigrants who left Northern Irish shores would be pioneers on account of the period in which they lived and the fact that new lands and colonies were in the process of development. Thus, in relation to one area of Pennsylvania, for example, a newspaper could, in poetic language, recount that:

So far as is known, the first white settlers in the valley were three brothers by the name of Chambers, from County Antrim, Ireland, sturdy men who had chosen the arduous life of the pioneer in the new Province of Pennsylvania. They first erected mills on the Fishing Creek, a tributary of the Susquehanna. The region was far from being uninhabited, for the wigwams of the Lenni-Lenapes were scattered all about; but there was plenty of room. There were open stretches of prairie, which invited the cultivation of grain and vegetables; herds of deer and bands of elk roamed freely through the forest, and the streams were full of fish. Penn's government had taught the Indians to respect the white man. The brothers were made welcome, and the most arable land was generously pointed out to them.[41]

But the Indians also told of a richer land further west, and the brothers paid close attention to this. In 1736 Benjamin Chambers built a log house which was the beginning of the town of Chambersburg. The *Weekly Telegraph* reported:

> New mills of various kinds were built, and other buildings followed; a garden and an orchard were planted. The adjacent country was rapidly settled by newcomers and a community of North of Ireland Presbyterians established itself, determining for all the future, the character of that part of Pennsylvania.[42]

Later emigrants would not be pioneers in the sense of pushing back territorial boundaries, but they would often show innovative spirit in other ways. David Ennis, who was born at Six Road Ends, Kircubbin, County Down, in 1839, would emigrate to the goldfields of Australia in 1856 and then move to New Zealand, where he had a 1,000 acre wheat farm and operated the first wire binder for sheaves. His brother William founded a township of Ennis in Madison Valley, Montana.[43] In the sense of becoming 'comfortable' there were undoubtedly success stories among the Ulster emigrants. Not all would be so successful; the father of future US President Andrew Johnston, for example, would be every bit as poor when he died in a drowning accident in Raleigh, North Carolina, as the family had been before leaving the North of Ireland, and Johnston himself, although he would rise to high office, started off his working life by running away from an apprenticeship and being unable to read and write until taught by his wife.[44] The missing relatives columns in provincial newspapers show that many emigrants did not maintain contact with home, although whether this relates to them falling on hard times and moving around frequently in search of employment is impossible to quantify without research. Examples include William Sims and Joseph Thompson Sims of Carrickfergus, one last heard of in the United States in 1873, the latter in Brisbane around the same time, where he was staying with a Belfastman named Sam Russell. In 1901 their sister Agnes Martin of Midland Street in Belfast was hoping to obtain information about them. At the same time Margaret McMullan of Alexander Street, Ballymena, was hoping for news of her brother William Sheals, a shoemaker, who left Ballymena in the early 1860s and was last heard of in Montreal in Canada. Such poignant entries in the 'Relatives Missing' column of the *Weekly Telegraph* point to broken links along the way. For some the reason for such a situation may have been inability to construct suitable letters, or perhaps disinterest in a home which lay a lifetime away.[45] Some may have moved from place to place to find employment and their intention to write home may have been superseded by distance and time as the journey progressed. There were others who did not forget their homeland, however, or, at any rate, family members still there. Documentation contained in an old court ledger from

Larne, for example, which turned up several years ago, reveal that when John Cunningham of Clark township, Ontario, died in 1871, he bequeathed part of his lands to his cousin Francis Wiles in County Antrim.[46]

In 1847 Harrison Allmond, Jr, of Norfolk, Virginia, sent ten pounds to James Barnett JP of the Carrickfergus Relief Fund for the assistance of the destitute of the district.[47] Several years earlier the will of former Larne man William Johnston was executed at Demerara in the West Indies, with the result that the not inconsiderable sum of £100 was donated in aid of the funds of the First Presbyterian congregation of the County Antrim town, a further £100 going to the Larne National Schools. A memorial plaque in the Old Presbyterian Church of Larne and Kilwaughter acknowledges the far-off benefactor.[48]

In many cemeteries I have visited in the United States there are clear instances of families remembering their origins. At the Upper Long Cane Cemetery in Abbeville County, South Carolina, I was amazed to find a stone with the motto 'Behold the Lamb' which was in memory of Mary C. Moore, wife of John Knox "Born in the town of Raloo, County Antrim, Ireland" Mary died at the age of 40 in July 1878, her husband followed her in March 1887[49]. Raloo is a rural area which has provided many American emigrants and the ancestors of at least two Presidents and a Vice President. The actual settlement of Raloo is a tiny clachan of houses and to see it described as a town was somewhat wide of the mark, but tribute nevertheless by the Moores and Knoxes to the place they had left behind them. Another aspect of this respect for the connections can be found in many cemeteries in Northern Ireland, where emigrants are mentioned on gravestones. A member of the Allen family in Philadelphia caused an impressive granite stone and plot surround to be erected in Templecorran cemetery, County Antrim, for example,[50] while the inscription on the Burrell gravestone in the little graveyard of Ballycarn near Drumbo was paid for by an exiled son to honour his parents. It states:

> Erected by Joseph Burrell of Yarmouth, Nova Scotia, in memory of his father Henry Burrell who died 8 February 1849 aged 70 years. And his mother Rosanna Burrell who died 12 September 1849 aged 72 years.[51]

The descendants of Ulster emigrants are undoubtedly considerable. Whenever the Barry family held a reunion at the old homestead of County Antrim settlers James and Susan Barry at Loch, Victoria, in 1989, some 96 descendants were present at that happy family event, including, at that time, the three remaining children of the 1921 migration. A similar story came from Hickory, Pennsylvania in 1984 when 600 descendants of Robert Lyle of Raloo gathered from 21 of the United States to mark the 200th anniversary of his arrival in America. The reunion had been happening since 1909, and asked by the local newspaper why they continued to hold it, those present cited the feeling of strong family ties and interest in their heritage.[52]

On occasions that heritage could be traced by the spread of local place names; there is a Newry in South Carolina, several Antrims, a Belfast and a Bangor in Maine, a New Londonderry in New Hampshire and a Mount Mourne in North Carolina, for example. Sometimes the names are more relevant to individuals, as was the case with Hugh McConnell, who named his home at Victoria in Australia 'Raloo' after the County Antrim district in which he had been born in 1858.[53]

In Laurens County in South Carolina the Belfast house is one of the oldest landmarks of historical interest and was built by the son of County Antrim emigrants. Colonel John Simpson (1751–1815) was the son of William and Mary Simpson, who emigrated to the United States with four of their five children. John apparently remained in Belfast to

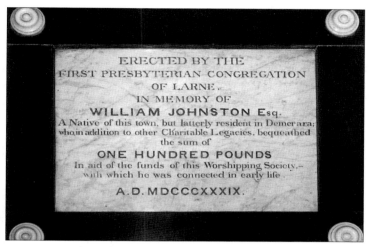

A plaque inside the Old Presbyterian Congregation of Larne and Kilwaughter commemorates the benevolence of William Johnston of the town, an emigrant to Demerara, and one of several from the area who made fortunes in the sugar trade.

William Cooper, County Librarian of Laurens County, South Carolina, at the Belfast house, which was built in 1786 by Colonel John Simpson, one of the many Ulster-Scots who settled the area, for his English bride, Mary Wells of Oxfordshire. The house, located in a rural part of the county, is one of the oldest and best preserved landmarks in the Piedmont section of South Carolina. It was the birthplace of William Dunlap Simpson, Governor of South Carolina 1879–80.

complete his education, and later became a merchant in London, marrying Mary Wells of Burford, Oxfordshire and, six weeks later, following the trail of his parents to South Carolina. He built a tall Georgian two and a half storey house constructed of brick made in Ireland – something which serves to indicate his prosperity. There were also hand-carved mantles of black walnut inside the house which were imported from England. The couple had four daughters and three sons, and became very prominent in the life of the district as well as South Carolina generally (one daughter married John Griffin, who served in the state House of Representatives, State Senate and US Congress, this latter between 1831–41).

There have been other instances of local place names being transplanted. Settlers from County Tyrone were responsible for the naming of Straban township in Pennsylvania, north of Gettysburg in the 18th century, early settlers having surnames such as Bell, Campbell, Dixon, Fleming, Hadden, Henderson, Maxwell, Miller, Murphy, McBroom, McCrea, Neely, Patterson, Reid, Ross and Simpson. Among them were John and Jean King, who were from Dungannon, and had originally settled in Tyrone Township, Adams County, Pennsylvania, and David Hunter, whose family roots lay in Londonderry, and who founded Hunterstown, an Ulster settlement in the midst of the homesteads scattered across the township.[54] Further north in Canada, on the North Bruce peninsula in Ontario, Alexander McNeill built a stately home modelled on and named in honour of his old childhood home, The Corran, at Larne Harbour, while also in Ontario another political figure like McNeill was Colonel TR Ferguson MP, who was born in Drumcor, County Cavan, in 1818 and settled in Cookstown, Ontario, an area with obvious local connection, in 1842.[55] The town of Fullerton, Louisiana, was named after the family of the same surname from Raloo in County Antrim, who were prominent in the lumber business and formed a company whose sales exceeded $6 million in 1931 – probably good enough reason to have a town named after the firm.[56]

There is still a Glenarm in Ontario, but Larne and Glenarm which used to be railway halts on the railroad line in Kentucky in the USA have long since disappeared, failing to function once the railway company collapsed and they became simply too isolated. One of the Orange lodges in Western Canada in the early 1900s – Magherafelt LOL 864 – obviously had some County Londonderry exiles involved.[57] An intriguing entry in a newspaper births column in 1867 informs us that the wife of Mr R McVeagh had given birth to a son at Larne Lodge, Cambridge, Waikato, New Zealand, but sadly we cannot glean who had built Larne Lodge or when they had left their native shores[58]. Often names remain in family folklore without a complete understanding as to the location which they commemorate. Several years ago a lady wrote to me of her ancestor, James Steen, who settled in South Carolina and fought at the revolutionary Battle of Kings Mountain. The interesting thing was, that although she had no idea where it was, family history had handed down the information over

The grave of Jane Boyd, one of the emigrants in the 1772 migration of Rev William Martin and his Covenanter Presbyterian congregations from Ulster. Those who sailed on the five ships formed an important and major element of Ulster-Scots in the Piedmont region of South Carolina.

generations that James Steen was from a place called the Vow in County Antrim. Steen descendants had never come back to County Antrim and did not even know where the rural district of the Vow was. But it symbolised that names had remained in the hearts of the emigrant community even if they never appeared on a map in their new worlds. Northern Ireland exiles might receive a surprise, however, on the South Island of New Zealand, where an isolated coastal settlement with half a dozen farmhouses lies close to Invercargill on the southern tip of the island. The three streets in the little settlement bring to mind an exile's home, and are called Larne Street, Carrickfergus Street and Antrim Street; proof if any were needed that there are few parts of the globe were Ulstermen and women have not been found in bygone generations[59].

The courthouse dominates the town centre of Laurens, South Carolina. One of the early families in the area were the Simpsons, who built the Belfast House of bricks imported from Ireland

[8]   see, for example, Jean Stephenson, Scotch-Irish Migration to South Carolina 1772, Virginia, 1971

[9]   Letter from Thomas Wright, Plumstead, Pennsylvania, to Thomas Greer, Dungannon, 1774, detailed in *Aspects of Irish Social History 1750–1800*, ed Crawford and Trainor, Belfast, 1984, p53

[10]   ibid., p53

[11]   Letter from William Faris, 1800, in the Public Record Office of Northern Ireland, T3073/1

[12]   Isabel Crozer, William Fee McKinney of Sentry Hill: his family and friends, Coleraine, 1985, p67

[13]   Ronnie Hanna, Land of the Free. Ulster and the American Revolution, Lurgan, 1992

[14]   This can cause some confusion in family trees since two children have carried the same Christian name.

[15]   Andrea Steen, Stoneboro, An Historical Sketch of a South Carolina Community, Spartanburg, South Carolina, 1993

[16]   James Barry, for example, encouraged to settle in Australia by an acquaintance named Wilson, later stood sponsor for other families from his neighbourhood. The story of the Barrys is dealt with elsewhere in this volume

[17]   Letters of James Houston home to Larne, held in the Public Record Office of Northern Ireland

[18]   Bruce Elliott, Irish Migrants in the Canadas. A New Approach, Kingston and Montreal, 1988#

[19]   *Belfast Weekly Telegraph*, February 21, 1931

[20]   *Larne Monthly Visitor*, December 1859

[21]   Terry Coleman, Passage to America, op cit

22 Janice Kennedy, 'Waves of Misery', The Ottawa Citizen, October 31, 1996

23 Belle McKinney Hays Swope, *History of The Middle Spring Presbyterian Church*, Newville, Pennsylvania, 1900, p47

24 ibid., p50–53

25 ibid., p28–32

26 Donald Harman Akenson, *The Irish Diaspora. A Primer*, Institute of Irish Studies, 1993

27 ships listing of passengers from Ireland to America 1804–1806, held in the Public Record Office for Northern Ireland

28 Laurens County records, list in the Public Record Office of Northern Ireland provided by Mrs Bernice George, Laurens, South Carolina, 1979

29 Roll #95, Laurens County lists

30 Jo Robert Owens and Ruth Dickson Thomas, 1850 Federal Census, York District, South Carolina, York, 1987

31 Margaret Watson, *Greenwood County Sketches, Old roads and early families*, Greenwood, South Carolina, 1970

32 Information from Colin Tweed, Milton, New Zealand; also article 'Descendant of Magheramorne and Islandmagee emigrants returns 'home'', *Larne Times*, August 18, 1998

33 see, for example, Carroll S Caldwell, *The Caldwell family of Spartanburg County, South Carolina*, Spartanburg, 1999

34 *Belfast News Letter*, September 7, 1869

35 *Belfast News Letter*, 1874

36 *Larne Times*, March 1909

37 *Weekly Telegraph*, January 18, 1936

38 *Larne Times*, April 7, 1949

39 Angus Martin, 'Nineteenth Century County Antrim Immigrant Families in the Burgh of Campbeltown', in *The Glynns*, Journal of the Glens of Antrim Historical Society, Volume 13, 1985

40 *Weekly Telegraph*, January 11, 1930

41 *Weekly Telegraph*, August 17, 1918

42 *Weekly Telegraph*, 'Three Brothers from Antrim', August 17, 1918

43 Coffey and Morgan, *Irish Families in Australia and New Zealand, 1788–1979*, Victoria, Australia, 1979

44 see Hans L Trefousse, *Andrew Johnston. A biography*, New York

45 *Weekly Telegraph*, October 12, 1901

46 Information in the possession of the author, from notes taken in a court ledger by Francis Wiles, who was clerk of the petty sessions in the town at that time

47 *Northern Whig*, July 1, 1847

48 *Belfast News Letter*, September 11, 1840

49 Authors notes, taken in Abbeville, South Carolina, 1993

50 Hume and Nelson, *The Templecorran Project*, Larne, 1994

51 RSJ Clarke, *Gravestone Inscriptions, Volume 3, County Down, Baronies of Upper and Lower Castlereagh* Belfast, 1969

52 *Pittsburgh Post Gazette*, July 30, 1984

53 *Larne Times*, May 1, 1947

54 Arthur Weaner, 'Straban Township, Adams County, Pennsylvania. Its Origins and Settlers', *Ulster Folklife*, Volume 8, 1962

55 Rev Stuart Acheson, 'The Scotch-Irish in Canada', in the Proceedings of the Scotch-Irish Congress, 1891, p210

56 *Larne Times*, March 4, 1993 (see also the chapter on business)

57 *Weekly Telegraph*, April 8, 1905; other Orange lodges with names from home in Canada included Clones, Enniskillen, Caledon and Cookstown.

58 *Belfast News Letter*, January 5, 1867

59 Information from Ron Murray, an Ulster exile now living in Wairarapa, New Zealand, 27 August 2003

How they went: Emigrant journeys recalled

Boston Harbour; the first sight emigrants on the ship *Friend's Goodwill* would have of the new land in which they wished to settle was very different than the modern view. The ship journeyed across the Atlantic between May and September, with 52 passengers.

On a September day in 1717 a small ship called the *Friend's Goodwill* reached the waters of Boston Harbour, arriving after an 18 week passage from the coast of Ireland and bringing emigrants who had boarded at Larne in County Antrim. The *Boston News Letter* reported that she had on board:

> . . . two and fifty souls, who have sustained very great hardships in their voyage; by contrary winds, being put to very short allowances, both of bread, water and meat, that it is a miracle they did not all perish; but Gods good Providence has often been visibly seen in their preservation; first in meeting a ship at sea that spared them some Provisions; & then by Dolphins & Sharks they catch'd, and by Rain Water sav'd on their Decks, and on the 26 of August last all like to be Swallowed up by a violent storm, the sailors being spent with hunger and thirst hardly able to navigate their vessel; one man died on board, and they had thoughts of casting lots who should be killed to be eaten, which thro' Mercy was prevented.[60]

It had been an eventful voyage, on a route which many others would ply in the years to come. The account of the *Friend's Goodwill* is significant as among the first voyages of emigrant ships to be detailed in the 18th century, and also because no ship's passenger list has survived the years. In a way the 52 passengers of the Friends Goodwill are symbolic as 'Unknown Passengers' of the great population movement which would see Ulster townlands drained of population in the 18th century.

In 1993 I sat, during a transatlantic flight, and looked out of the window of the jet in which I was travelling to the sea far below. The few ships which we did see were tiny, and white sea horses were visible on the surface of the water. Some time later, flying close to Canada, ice floes were clearly visible. A matter of a few hours from Belfast and we landed at New York, into the midst of a bustling airport where thousands swept through the terminal buildings, different colours and nationalities briefly mixing before moving on. It was something of a metaphor for emigration generally. In the plane it had been amazing to think that once the seas had been plied, on the same route, but in a much slower fashion, by tiny emigrant ships such as the *Friend's Goodwill*, those on board setting their eyes firmly westward, to the future. At that time I was on a journey on behalf of a local authority interested in pursuing twinning links in South Carolina. I knew a lot about the emigrant routes and some of those who emigrated themselves. But nothing prepared me for the sight of the mighty Atlantic from several thousand feet, or the numerous sites which I would visit which spoke volumes of the emigrant trail from Ulster. This was not, however, a cold trail. In the Carolinas, as in many other parts of the world, the living legacy of emigration remained and was to be found in the modern descendants of those who left their homes in the north of Ireland for what they hoped would be a better life in a new land.

During my travels on that occasion I visited the town of Kingstree in South Carolina, situated in Williamsburg County, which had owed its foundation to settlers from Knockbracken in County Down in the 1730s. Behind the neon signs and the bustle in Kingstree we found a quiet corner reserved for the memory of the Witherspoons of Ulster and those who travelled with them across the Atlantic and up the Black River to their new homes. Theirs is just one of hundreds of stories in the Carolinas, Virginia, Tennessee, Pennsylvania and elsewhere of emigrant families and individuals from Northern Ireland, but it is a special story because one of the family wrote down his memories in later life, in a document known as *The Witherspoon Chronicle*.

For young Robert Witherspoon the story began on 14 September 1734 when a family group from Knockbracken, outside Belfast, went on board a ship in the lough which was to take them on the first stage of an epic journey across the Atlantic to the Carolinas. Two years before others from the same community and belonging to the same family network had undertaken the journey, encouraged by John Witherspoon, a patriarchal figure who had been born in Glasgow, and his wife Janet. Their emigration would actually occur in three phases over six years, and would take an extended family group to the town of Kingstree in South Carolina, and to the counties of Williamsburg and Orangeburg which surround it. [61]

There is a plaque in honour of the Witherspoons in the centre of the cemetery in Kingstree, which lies south east of Columbia, the state capital. At the Williamsburg Presbyterian Church, of which John was one of the founders, another plaque inside commemorates the role in the community which he played. I met church historians and officials there whose pride in their Ulster connection was clearly very deeply and sincerely held. Kingstree is a typical US small town, and

South Carolina residents Anne and Boyd Strawn at the memorial to the County Down emigrant John Witherspoon who was one of the founders of Kingstree and a leading light of the Williamsburg Presbyterian Church.

at the cemetery shady glades shelter the stones of generations of residents, the first families of them including the Wilsons, James', McDonalds, Armstrongs and Witherspoons. In the peace and the stillness, it is difficult to image the adventure and the uncertainty of the journey that took them from the old world to the new.

Fortunately one of the party, Robert Witherspoon, who was a young boy at the time, would later write down his memory of the voyage and the early months in America. *The Witherspoon Chronicle* provides a detailed and fascinating account of an Ulster emigrant group. [62]

Robert informs us that they went on board the ship on 14 September, but lay wind-bound in Belfast Lough for some 14 days. As if this was not enough of an ordeal, once the ship did set sail, disaster struck; Janet Witherspoon, Robert's grandmother, died at sea and was buried in the ocean, something which he describes as "an affective sight to her offspring". Worse, as Robert detailed, was to come:

> We were sorely tossed at sea with storms which caused our ship to spring a leek. Our pumps were kept incessantly at work day and night, for many days our mariners seemed many a time at their wits end, but it pleased God to bring us all safe to land, which was about the 1st of December.

Landing in Charles Town (now Charleston, South Carolina), the Ulster group found the local citizens very kindly disposed to them. No doubt those who had met them were even more sympathetic because of a second bereavement which took place after they arrived; Robert's sister Sarah had died in Charleston and been the first to be buried at the Scotch Meeting House graveyard. With the loss of two close family members en route, the Witherspoons must have been despondent as they made their journey to land plots further inland. The family remained in Charles Town, however, until after Christmas 1734, when they would set out in an open boat, along with tools and a year's provisions, to be conveyed along a waterway called the Black River to a landing at Potato Ferry. From that point they were on foot and in search of temporary shelter.

Robert, who finally wrote down his memoirs in 1780, recounted:

> Our provisions was (sic) Indian corn, rice, wheaten flours, beef, pork, rum and salt. We were much distressed in this part of air passage, as it was the dead of winter we were exposed to the inclemency of the weather day and night.

Fortunately, the first group of settlers – 47 in total, led by one Roger Gordon – had arrived two years before, in October

Williamsburg Presbyterian Church, founded by a group of County Down settlers in the 1730s. They named the church after William of Orange and the local counties are named Williamsburg and Orangeburg as a result.

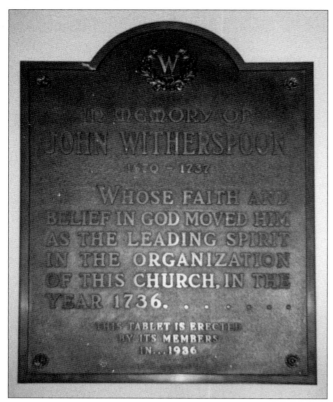

A memorial plaque inside Williamsburg Presbyterian Church to John Witherspoon, who was born in Glasgow and lived at Knockbracken, County Down, prior to leading an emigration from the area to South Carolina in 1732–36.

1732, and could offer shelter for the new arrivals. They slept in the barn of Samuel Commander while dirt houses were erected by the men, and Robert details that this new land with its extensive woods was "very severe of women and children". The next morning the family group set out again, and that evening they were dispersed to the homes of settlers with surnames such as McDonald, Plowden and Armstrong. William James Witherspoon, one of Robert's uncles, also hosted some of the new arrivals. "Their little cabins were as full that night as they could hold and the next day every one made the best they could to their own place, which was the 1st day of February", Robert recalled.

Following the loss of her mother-in-law and daughter, Elizabeth McQuoid, Robert's mother, hoped for "an agreeable place to live". Their first impressions were to be somewhat different, the Chronicle tells us:

> . . . when we arrived and saw nothing but a wilderness and instead of a fine timbered house, nothing but a very mean dirt house, our spirits quite sank . . . My father gave us all the comfort he could by telling us we would get all these trees cut down and in a short time there would be plenty of inhabitants, that we could see from house to house.

At that point a major domestic disaster took place. Fires were often carried by early settlers in metal boxes inside a wooden container. The Witherspoons had brought theirs from a place called Bog Swamp and it went out. The consequences were not only a lack of warmth, for their rude shelter had no door and there were wild animals in the forest which could attack them if there was not a fire blazing to scare them off. James Witherspoon decided on immediate action. Although he did not know the landscape, he followed the swamp upriver until he came to a branch, from which he found the farm of Roger Gordon. His family had watched him depart, then went back inside their hut, anxious and worried that they might never see him again. There was, no doubt, considerable celebration when he returned some time later with fire. His arrival was none too soon; as night fell they listened to the howl of wolves nearby. The large fire they burned to keep the wild beasts away compensated for the lack of any gun, no dog, and not even a door to their little hut.

The next morning was clear and warm, but a thunderstorm blew up, with thunder and lightning, and rain that washed through the roof of their hut. Robert tells us in his account: "I believe we all sincerely wished ourselves again at Belfast, but this fright was soon over and the evening cleared up comfortable and warm."

Some planting was done in the little Ulster farmsteads, although the season was now short, and moving around was difficult as swamps and branches of rivers had to be followed as guides to avoid becoming lost:

> People were much opprest in bringing their things, as there was no other way but to carry them on their backs, which consisted of the bed clothing, chist (chest), provisions, pots and tools, since at that time there were few or no roads.

In addition to the wild animals they had to contend with, there was anxiety over the Indians, although they faced no threat at this time. Robert sums up the early experience at the Bluff, their new home:

> When they (the Indians) came to hunt in the spring they were in great numbers in all places like the Egyptian Locusts but they were not hurtful. We had a great deal of trouble and hardships in our first setting but the few inhabitants continued yet in health and strength. Yet we were still opprest with fear on divers accounts, especially of being massacred by the Indians or bit by the snakes or torn by wild beasts or being lost or perished in the woods. Of the lost there was three persons.

Landmarks in the Witherspoon settlement included the arrival of his Uncle Robert from Belfast in 1736 on the ship *New Built*, and the arrival of the Rev Robert Herron from Ireland to minister to the settlement for three years. In 1737 John Witherspoon, the man whose idea the emigration was, died of a fever and was the first person to be buried at Williamsburg Meeting House.

Robert, his grandson and author of *The Witherspoon Chronicle*, had been born on 20 August 1728, in County Down and recounts how his father taught him to weave as a young boy. The family lived at the Bluff in Williamsburg County until March 1749 when they moved to another location known as Thorn Tree. Robert was a weaver and then became an overseer with the Flemming family near Black River Church, returning home after an outbreak of distemper claimed his eldest brother David and sister Jane. Robert remained on the family plantation until 1758, taking care of affairs for his parents, his father being in ill health. On 2 March 1758 he married Elizabeth Heathly, who was then 18 years of age. Their son James was born in 1759, Thomas was born in 1761, Ann was born in 1763, John was born in 1774. A second Thomas was born in July 1776, taking the name of his brother who, along with John, had died as young children. In 1767 a new Robert Witherspoon also entered the world.

When Elizabeth McQuoid Witherspoon died on 25 January 1777 in the 72nd year of her age, it was the end of an era: she was the last surviving branch of the old stock of the family which had journeyed the great distance from Knockbracken and Drumbo to the other side of the world.

In his remarks Robert Witherspoon accords them tribute:

> I bear them this testimony, that they were much in prayer, they were strict observers of the Sabbath, in a word they were a stock that studied outward piety and inward purity, indeed God blessed this settlement at first with a number of godly pious men out of which I choose to set down some of their names – William Wilson, David Allen, William Hamilton, John Porter, William James, David Wilson, John James, James McCollond, Robert Pressly, James Bradley, John Lemon, William Frierson, to which l add my own father and my three uncles (viz David, Robert and Gavin). They were men of great piety in their day and indeed they were men of renown.

The settlement would grow and prosper as the Rev James Wallace noted in 1856:

> Immediately after their arrival they laid out the town of Williamsburg, on the site of the present village of Kingstree, which they named in honour of William III, Prince of Orange . . . But one of the first cares of this pious colony was to build a house to the Lord. [63]

So many other congregations were, in fact, to be founded by families who originated in Williamsburg that the congregation is regarded as the Mother Church of Presbyterianism in South Carolina.

The petition for land for a church and manse was presented by William James, who had been an officer in the Williamite army, and the first three ministers – Revs Herron, Ray and Kennedy – were from Ireland. Williamsburg Presbyterian Church not only grew, but other churches including lndiantown Presbyterian seventeen miles away, with Wilsons and James' predominant, also were established from

the original congregation members.[64] The Indiantown church is picturesquely situated a few miles away from Kingstree, having been founded in or around 1756, and was the oldest 'offspring' of the Williamsburg congregation. Among the first elders were Robert Wilson, who had been an elder of the Williamsburg church, and Major John James, who came to South Carolina with his family in the first County Down migration to the area in 1732. His father William was said to have served with the Williamite forces at the Battle of the Boyne, and Major John James would play a significant role in the Indiantown community during the American Revolution.

John and Janet Witherspoon, meanwhile, were cousins, and both had been born in Scotland around 1670. They lived their younger years in or near Glasgow and in 1695 moved from Scotland to Ireland settling, like many others in the post-Williamite War period, in the province of Ulster, in their case in the county of Down, and parish of Drumbo. Robert says that his grandfather ". . . lived in good circumstances and in good credit until the year 1734 he moved with his family to South Carolina."

Robert himself was the son of James Witherspoon, John's second son and third child of seven. James was born

Indiantown Presbyterian Church in South Carolina. The church was founded by members of Williamsburg Church and was to be burnt down by troops during the American Revolution because members of the congregation formed a unit known as 'The Swamp Foxes' to support the Patriot cause.

around the turn of the 17th century into the 18th and lived at Drumbo until he was 25, when he married 20 year-old Elizabeth McQuoid, whose mother was a Campbell. James and Elizabeth settled at Grabo (Greyabbey) Parish near the Cunning Burn Mill, living there for nine years before joining the extraordinary emigration of their family. James sold his tenantry and took his family to Knockbracken in May, leaving to work in the reed making business himself until September 1734.

Those who made the journey across the Atlantic included Janet Witherspoon, John's daughter, who was married to John Flemming, or Fleming, in Ireland and they brought seven children – Isabella, John, Elizabeth, James, Janet, Penelope and William. John Flemming died in 1750, Janet in 1761 at the age of 66 years. David Witherspoon and his wife Ann Pressley brought their children Sarah and Janet on the journey (interestingly these Pressley's may be ancestral relations of Elvis, according to the belief of some in South Carolina that the King of Rock and Roll was of Scotch-Irish descent). Elizabeth Witherspoon and her husband William James came with their children Mary, Janet, John and William. Robert Witherspoon's wife had died and he had married Hester Jane Scott a short time before they emigrated with two children, Mary and John. David Wilson and Mary Witherspoon brought their children William and John with them.

Robert Witherspoon was quite literally at the centre of the County Down settlements in Williamsburg and Orangeburg counties. He arrived in 1734, an earlier settlement had established itself in 1732 and a third would arrive in 1736. But in his decision to write an extensive personal account of the trials and endeavours of his family, Robert Witherspoon handed down to posterity the story of an epic journey by tenacious men, women and children.

Thankfully his is not the only account of emigrant voyages which have survived. Another which relates to South Carolina is the journal of John Blair, who sailed from Larne on a ship called the *Sally*, of Savannah in Georgia, in April 1796. John Blair's Journal is now a document in the keeping of the University of South Carolina at Columbia,[65] and is a fascinating account which concerns itself with the voyage across the Atlantic. Blair tells us that on Thursday, 21 April 1796:

> . . . they lifted the anchor and got her underway about 15 minutes after I had come on board, so that I nearly missed my passage, from my attention to conveying friends who had been on board to see me...the leaving of my native country, perhaps forever, left me melancholy as we charted the North Channel.

Blair continues to outline the events of the voyage:

> On the second day the vessel has a considerable motion and I find myself somewhat sick . . . 23 April 1796, I was extremely sick this day, as were the rest of the passengers in general.

The next day things were no better, and the author of the Journal relates "violent and frequent vomitting (sic)", with a good number of the passengers sharing his views that it would be better to be back home again. Things would improve, however, and by 29 April John recounted that they had voyaged 209 miles, although he was not overly impressed with this, which was a sixteenth of the journey. By the next day fresh breezes encouraged the prospect of 'a good passage' and 141 miles had been covered en route to Charleston in South Carolina. By 2 May, the Journal tells us that:

> . . . these 24 hours fine favourable fresh gales. At 10am they set the square main sail. We have now a reasonable hope of a good passage, as we have made these three days 460 miles, which is more than double the distance we made the first week, and should this favourable gale continue, we could make Charleston in less than 18 days.

However it is clear from the Journal that there were tensions building up among the passengers and a scuffle broke out on 5 May over whose turn it was to heat their pot on the fire for supper; "This obliged us to make a code of laws to prevent such trouble in future," John Blair related. The next day he and Henry McNeill, another passenger, devised a code of conduct to help "preserve the peace of the vessel". The passengers unanimously agreed to these and a committee of six men was set up to whom redress could be made if grievances occurred in future.

With the journey almost nearing completion, on Sunday, 12 June, Blair could write that the coast of North Carolina was in sight and they could see the trees there. On 17 June the ship was within two miles of the land which "has a fine fragrant smell and a beautiful appearance". There was still a distance to be covered, however, and contrary winds were unhelpful to the *Sally*. On 23 June the captain of the ship

Roy Blair of Union County, South Carolina, a descendant of John Blair who left an account of his journey across the Atlantic in 1796.

introduced half rations of the food supply, including bread, butter and molasses, a measure which provoked considerable grumbling among the passengers. Any doubts about the continued hazards of the journey, however, were brought home a week later when a thunderstorm struck around eleven in the evening. The foreyard and main stay-sail were broken and damaged in the storm, and some of the lightning which occurred came close to the quarter deck.

It was, as it transpired, the last drama to be played out on the ocean. On Thursday, 7 July 1796, amid light breezes and clear weather, the passengers of the *Sally* began to bring up their bundles of clothes, in preparation for their arrival the next day in Charleston. John Blair would be the founder of quite a dynasty in the southern and western United States. Born in County Tyrone, he settled at Yorkville, South Carolina (now York), where he died in 1848,[66] by which time emigrant ships were of a higher standard and the voyage times doubtless somewhat quicker, but the hazards of the weather and the mercy of the elements remained the same.

Robert Pillow, from Mullabane outside Armagh city, who emigrated to Australia in 1852, details how his journey from Belfast in the steamer *Tynwald* in December that year saw a stormy passage to Liverpool. On Christmas Day, 1852, he was on board the ship *Digby*, anchored in the Liverpool Basin. Pillow recorded that day:

> Blowing a gale, was obliged to let go the second anchor as the one already down was dragging; the wind increased to a hurricane and for several days after ships arrived in a disabled condition. One large ship was towed in and anchored near ours that had lost all above her decks with the exception of her lower masts.[67]

The start of the voyage did not augur well, for the ship's anchors had become entangled during the storm and it proved impossible to lift them. The vessel sailed on, but near the mouth of the Mersey the anchors struck under the *Digby* and had to be let go, a misfortune added to by the breaking of the rope to the tug which was assisting them to the sea. The small tug was unable to approach the ship owing to the heavy seas and the *Digby* twice touched sandbanks, although fortunately managed to get clear on both occasions. The weather continued to be wild until mid-January, as the *Digby* and her passengers began their journey down the Irish Sea. En route they had a last view of the northern Irish coast, Dundrum Bay and St John's Point being clearly visible to the 318 passengers, who included emigrants from Antrim, Tyrone and Armagh.[68] The voyage was not to be without incident, and was faithfully recorded by Pillow. He tells of the dangers of the ship almost being driven ashore on the Spanish coast and of the concerns about pirate ships, with an unidentified vessel having passed close by in the night at one time, while the passengers armed themselves and prepared to help defend the *Digby* if needed.

Unity of purpose there may have been on that occasion, but as the journey continued tensions developed among the emigrants. The author tells us that one of those on board was accused of beating his wife, found guilty by a special court established on the vessel and received 12 bucketfuls of water over his head. This was not the end of the matter, however, for later in the evening he attacked one of his chief accusers, who returned to the deck with a pistol and was disarmed and placed in irons for a day. It was probably fortunate that the arrival of a barque with government emigrants bound for Australia brought a new drama; a ship's doctor was needed because two of those on board were ill and their ship's doctor had died. The vessel, the *Sacramento*, was later found to have run aground on rocks on the Australian coast, and although the passengers and crew were all saved, they lost their luggage and the ship broke up – a clear example of the dangers involved in many an emigrant voyage.

For Pillow and his fellow passengers, a safe arrival in Melbourne occurred on 29 April – but only after they had paid extra to be landed there. There had been no deaths and little sickness during the voyage from Liverpool. He detailed that:

> We amused ourselves in various ways during the voyage – we had sham parliaments; many sham trials and one real

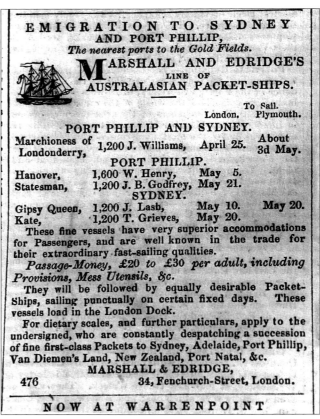

An advertisement in the Northern Whig of 1853 offering emigrants the chance to sail to Sydney and Port Phillip in Australia, "the nearest ports to the Gold Fields".

one; singing, music, and dancing on deck in fine weather; fishing for fish and birds; shooting birds and fish with guns and pistols of all kinds; swimming in the sea on calm days; reading, playing chess, cards and drafts; looking out for land, ships, whales, sharks, porpoises, etc.[69]

At least some of those who undertook the emigrant journey in the 19th century were lured by that most exceptional economic imperative – the quest for gold. In 1852 another Ulster emigrant had arrived in Melbourne, his account of his journey to the gold fields being carried (although his name was not) by the *Northern Whig* the following January. In a letter home to friends in Belfast, he related how a journey of 120 miles had taken him from Melbourne to the gold 'diggings'[70] The account gives a detailed idea of what life in the goldfields was like:

> You are dressed with a large pair of boots, which come over the knees; a blue flannel shirt, which acts as a coat; and a belt around your waist, on which are strung your quart pot and pannikin; and upon your back is what they call here a 'snagg', comprising your blankets, quilt, shirts, socks, tea, coffee, sugar and any other little things you may require to bring. You always 'bush it', that is sleep out, with the sky for your roof; you choose a dry place, rig up a tent with some of your blankets, light a fire, boil your tea (with no milk, of course) and take some dry bread to it; then you may sit up as long as you wish, or repair, not to a downy couch, but to a bed of boughs off a tree, with all your wearing clothes on excepting your boots. I never had my clothes off for the six weeks I was away.

The account continued to detail that:

> You rise about daybreak, make your breakfast, strike your tent, and start upon your journey. I could not convey to you an idea of the roads here, for they are made through the open country, and the tremendous traffic upon them makes them in a bad state. I never was a day travelling on them but I was up to the waist either in muck or water before night. The rivers through the country have no bridges, of course, and I have crossed them not half-an-hour after men have been drowned in them making the attempt, having been swept off their feet owing to the force of the water coming down after a night's rain.

It took about five days to travel to the diggings, the account tells us, and the gold diggers sank a hole about six feet diameter in the ground, digging down until they came to a clay-pipe bottom, which was where gold was to be found. The sinking averaged about thirty to forty feet while a seam of two to eighteen inches was where the lucky prospector found gold.

While some did very well indeed on the goldfields, others, such as the author of the account, fared less well. He related how he had hurt his hand through the pick work which was required and had been forced to return to Melbourne having only obtained a little more than covered his expenses. Fortunately he was able to obtain work in a wine and spirit store as a clerk, but complained of the cost of living and did not recommend emigration owing to the expense of living there and the fact that "Lodgings can scarcely be got here for love or money."

There can be little doubt that life for the emigrant was not an easy one in the early years of his or her arrival. Those taking ship for America often went as indentured servants, paying for the cost of their voyage through effectively signing away their freedom in the New World for four or five years, the ship's captain obtaining as much as he could at the dockside for their labour. As was the case to a lesser extent at the hiring fairs in Ulster, the labourer was very much at the mercy of the employer, who could be kind or otherwise depending on fortune.

When the Stewart family left Whiteabbey in the earlier part of the 19th century and sailed to Quebec they found farmhouses showing the appearance of both prosperity and comfort. What they did not realise at the time was that the settlers concerned had been five years building up their resources to arrive at that point.[71] The Stewarts were, however, probably better off than many emigrants, even though a manufacturing business with which they had been involved in County Antrim had failed. They obtained a land grant of 12,000 acres each in the township of Douro, near the present city of Peterborough, Ontario. But they nevertheless found the same problems besetting them as occurred for many early settlers; in February 1823 they arrived to find their new house in the midst of a snowstorm. Mrs Francis Browne Stewart wrote:

> The door had not yet been hung or any partitions erected. Where the chimney was to be, was a large opening in the roof. The floor was covered with ice and mortar.[72]

One of the common complaints for many new settlers in the Carolinas had been the onset of fever and malaria, which claimed many lives. In Ontario the Stewarts found they were also susceptible to illness, with Thomas Alexander Stewart succumbing for a time to 'lake fever', described as "the pest of the new settlers".

Despite all the many problems of the voyage, the journey and the settling in, and sometimes the loss of family members along the way, as happened with Samuel McCulloch of Carrickfergus in 1774 and the Witherspoons in the 1734 emigration from Knockbracken, Ulster emigrants proved resilient people. Thomas A Stewart, to cite one example, died in 1847, and was survived by some 22 children and grandchildren. His wife lived on until February 1872, passing away at the age of 78 years. Not only did they prove stubborn and tenacious, but they were also, as President Theodore Roosevelt had it, a virile race[73]. From early pioneers, and their settlements, would spring many descendants and much input into the life and spirit of the communities around them. There are many parts of the world which owe a considerable amount in their development and in their outlook and ethos to the presence of settler families from the Ulster counties.

The late Mrs Hellene Carlisle (centre), church historian of Nazareth Presbyterian Church, Spartanburg, who did much to preserve the memory of Ulster families who settled the area and founded the congregation, with fellow enthusiasts CC Caldwell of Greer, South Carolina, and his late wife Harriet. The congregation was founded in the 18th century by families with surnames including Anderson, Barry, Caldwell, Crawford, Hadden, Moore, Reid and others, all from County Antrim.

[60] *Boston News Letter*, from Monday 9 September to 16 September 1717, American Antiquarian Society microprints

[61] The counties of Williamsburg and Orangeburg, and Williamsburg Presbyterian Church, were named in honour of William, Prince of Orange, on whose behalf at least one of the group had fought during the Battle of the Boyne in 1690.

[62] The 'Witherspoon Chronicle' is contained in the *History of Williamsburg Presbyterian Church 1736–1981*, Kingstree 1981.

[63] Williamsburg Presbyterian Church history

[64] *History of Indiantown Presbyterian Church 1757–1957*, Indiantown, South Carolina, 1957, p7

[65] John Blair's Journal, University of South Carolina, Columbia, archives

[66] *Belfast News Letter*, 27 December 1848, states that "(Died) At Yorkville, South Carolina, on 3rd October last, Captain John Blair, aged 78 years. He was born in county Tyrone – spent the early part of his life in Strabane and Donagheady, and emigrated to America in 1796" Today Blair's descendants are scattered across the southern and western United States – information from Roy F Blair, Union, South Carolina.

[67] TGF Patterson, 'Account of a voyage to Australia in 1852', in *Ulster Folklife*, Volume 8, 1962

[68] Those listed include James Martin and Samuel McClinton, Moy, County Tyrone, Mrs Dinsmore and son, Jenetta McCready, Portrush, Messrs Rutherford, Mains, Foy, Edward Kennedy, County Antrim, two Ferguson brothers from Glenarm, Thomas Crighton and his brother 'from the north', Samuel Pillow, wife and child and brother Robert, Mullabane, Armagh.

[69] Patterson, op cit, p87

[70] The account appears in the *Northern Whig* of 22 January 1853

[71] 'Ulster family who became pioneers in Canada', *Larne Times*, 13 July 1945

[72] ibid., *Larne Times*, 13 July 1945

[73] Roosevelt is himself believed to have had Ulster ancestry among his family tree, and there is a plaque in Gleno, County Antrim, commemorating these links

Back to the land: Farming folk who found a new future in far-off lands

The Barry family of James and Sarah and their children James, William, Wilson, Mary, Anna, Susan and John. This photograph was taken in Larne prior to their emigration to Victoria, Australia, in 1921.

courtesy The Barry family, Australia

The scene must have been a poignant one, as members of the Barry family loaded up horses and carts to take their belongings six miles through the rural countryside near Larne to the harbour, and a boat which would take them to Scotland. They were leaving behind their farm holding on the heights of an Antrim hillside overlooking the North Channel, and their hopes were for a new life on the land elsewhere. The testimony to their tenacity is the fact that their modern descendants own and farm hundreds of acres of land accumulated by the family through hard work over the generations since the 1920s.

Their neighbours and friends had given them beds the night before, and as they slowly made their way along the hill road at Magheramorne and saw the harbour in the distance they must have had mixed feelings. James and Susan Barry would have been hopeful of a new future, but also anxious about the long journey with their seven children. Their children would have been sorry to leave their home and their friends, but also excited about an epic journey to the other side of the world. Their neighbours watched them go and one of them, William Hume of Monterloney Farm, had written a song for his neighbour James Barry. James had packed it in his luggage, its chorus reminding him for years to come of that final departure:

> Farewell to the green fields of Erin
> farewell to the land I was born
> farewell to Aul Wassagh, Ballyedward
> and the dear friends of sweet Magheramorne

Although the Barry children would not know it then, some of them and many of their descendants would time and again retrace the steps of that journey and come back to their old homeland to view the sites that James and Susan Barry would never see again. All that was in the future, however, for a long journey awaited them to a new world under the Southern Cross. They were bound for South Gippsland, Victoria.

The decision of James and Susan Barry to emigrate to South Gippsland, was spurred by a man named Bob Wilson[74]. He had settled at Krowera, near Loch, and on a return visit to his native Ireland recommended to the Barrys that they come to Australia to find a new life of prosperity. The land which they farmed at Ballyedward comprised 40 acres, and they would have known the problems of trying to sustain a family of seven children on such a small acreage. It may not have been the best of land, since the song *James Barry's Farewell* refers to 'McKinty's aul barren wet spot' as being the location. It could not have been, easy, however, to decide on emigration from family and friends, but they sold their two properties at Bankhall and paid for their passage to Australia, the sum involved being £260, a considerable amount in the early 1920s.

The journey to Stranraer from Larne was the shortest to be undertaken as part of the emigration. From the Scottish port they took a train south to London, and on 10 February 1921, boarded a ship at Southampton. Six weeks later, on 23 March, the liner, which James later informed friends in a letter home, had 1500 passengers aboard, docked at Portmelbourne harbour in Australia[75].

William Barry, aged 13, had contacted Diphtheria and spent three weeks in the ship's hospital and a further four weeks in a hospital, and Susan Barry and the remainder of the family stayed in Melbourne with a Mrs Lawerance while her husband accompanied Mr Wilson to the Loch district seeking employment and accommodation for his family. When the Barrys first arrived in the township of Loch they stayed in a house in Smith Street, and they later lived on a farm at Jeetho near Loch for a year while they share-farmed for a Mr McCabe; undertaking the work on the farm earned them two-fifths of the proceeds. James Barry then moved to a farm at Loch, and a dairy herd was built up on the leased property.

Like many emigrants, they faced difficult times and in a recollection at the 75th Barry Family Reunion in March 1996, one of the Barry children, Wilson, (then 84) spoke of how the time came when the interest on the property could not be paid because of the depression:

> Mr McCabe came around to collect it. Mother answered the knock at the door and knew very well what he had come for. She broke down, poor mother. She was as honest as the day was long and to think she couldn't pay her debt or interest rate, she just broke down. It softened the old man's heart and he turned on his heels and went back home[76].

The Barrys were not the only family suffering through the depression years and the Australian government brought in a moratorium which eased the burden of paying interest, allowing people to pay what they could afford without the danger of them being thrown off their property for default. It would have been an anxious time, but the economy of the country improved and the Barry's eventually paid for their land. What stood them in good stead, Wilson Barry said, was that they were seen to be improving the farm, getting it cleared and into grass pasture, and making it productive. Times were changing for the better, emphasised by the purchase in 1924 of 255 acres along the Wonthaggl Road, Loch. This latter property, which was added to the Bladen farm they were already leasing, became known as Ashton and became home to their herd of 16 cattle at that time. It was named after one of their old family homes in County Antrim.

In 1944 Ashton was divided into three separate farms. James and Susan would live on 50 acres known as Homeleigh, while James Jnr and William and their families lived on the remainder. Whenever the County Antrim pioneers passed away they left Homeleigh to their youngest daughter, Anna, who was a spinster and had nursed them during the latter stages of their lives. Anna, who was just five when the family sailed from Lame, had trained as a nurse in the Ballarat Base Hospital and then as a midwife at the Queen Victoria Hospital in Melbourne. She was matron of Korumburra Hospital for many years, and was an infant welfare sister of the district from 1958 until she retired in 1978. Anna never married and she passed away at Korumburra in 1992.

An obituary article which appeared in a South Gippsland newspaper on Tuesday 16 June 1992, noted:

> . . . she became the friend and confidante to many concerned young mothers, and made herself available at all times to those who needed her advice or just someone to listen to their worries. Several young men in the shire were, as new-born babies, named 'Barry' by grateful parents.[77]

Anna was one of the original Barry emigrant children who were alive, in 1989, for a unique family celebration to mark the 68th anniversary of their safe arrival in Australia. She and her other brother, Wilson, presided over a gathering of 96 descendants of the original family group, and an exhibition of

THE ABERDEEN LINE.

No. 180 *Managers:* **GEO. THOMPSON & CO., Ltd., 7, Billiter Square, London, E.C. 3.**

CONTRACT TICKET.
(TRANSFERABLE).

NOTICE.

Your attention is specially di
to the conditions of transportat
the annexed contract.

The Company do not
liability for loss of or damage to b
but passengers can protect them
by insurance.

...ting a Passage as a Third Class (Steerage) Passenger in any ship proceeding from the British ...erranean Sea, immediately on the payment or deposit by such Third Class (Steerage) Passenger ...ject of the Passage engaged.
...he Ticket.
...inted in plain and legible characters and legibly signed with the Christian Names and Surname
...rk must be inserted in Words, and not in Figures.
...nger, nor any Alteration, Addition, or Erasure made in it.
...tipulation, or exception not contained in this form.

"...S" of 11,223 Tons Register, to take in Passengers at the
...IA on the_____day of_____1920
...rgin shall be provided with a Third Class (Steerage) Passage to,
and shall be Landed at the Port of___MELBOURNE___in___AUSTRALIA___in the Steam Ship "DEMOSTHENES" with not less than Fifteen Cubic Feet for Luggage for each Statute Adult, and shall be victualled during the voyage and the time of detention at any place before its termination, according to the subjoined Scale, for the sum of £ *200* including Government Dues before embarkation, and head money, if any, at the place of landing, and every other charge except Freight for excess of Luggage beyond the quantity above specified, and I hereby acknowledge to have received the sum of £ *130* in {full/part} payment.

The luggage carried under this engagement, whether in excess of Fifteen Cubic Feet or not, shall be deemed to be of a value not exceeding £10, unless the value in excess of that sum be declared and paid for. The Ship shall have liberty to comply with any orders or directions as to departure, arrival, routes, ports of call, stoppages, or otherwise howsoever given by His Majesty's Government or any Department thereof or any person acting or purporting to act with the authority of His Majesty or of His Majesty's Government or of any Department thereof or by any Committee or person having, under the terms of the War Risks Insurance on the Ship, the right to give such orders or directions, and if by reason of and in compliance with any such orders or directions anything is done or is not done the same will not be deemed a deviation.

The following quantities, at least, of Water and Provisions will be supplied by the Master of the Ship as required by Law, viz. : Four Quarts daily to each Statute Adult, exclusive of the quantity necessary for cooking any article issued under this scale, in a cooked state.

NAMES.	Ages.	No. of Statute Adults
Mr. J. Barry	40	
Mrs. S. do	38	
Mary do	15	
William do	13	
Sarah do	11	
Wilson do	9	
Jack do		
Annie J. do		3
James do		

Provisions Weekly per Statute Adult.

	Lbs. Ozs.		Lbs. Ozs.
Beef or Pork	2 4	Raisins	0 6
Preserved Meat	1 0	Tea	0 2
Sugar		Sugar	1 0
Bread or Biscuit		Salt	0 2
Wheaten Flour		Mustard	0 0½
Oatmeal, Rice and Peas		Pepper, ground	0 0½
Potatoes		Dried or Compressed Veg.	0 0
		Vinegar or Pickles	1 gill

Bedding and Table Requisites are provided by the Ship.

For OSCAR STEPHEN THOMPSON,

To be signed in full by the person issuing the Ticket.} ___*D.E. Humphreys*___

7, BILLITER SQUARE, LONDON, E.C. 8.

Date of Issue ___**15 NOV 1920**___ 192

Deposit ......£ *130*

Balance......£ *180* to be paid at 7, Billiter Square, London, three days prior to Embarkation,

Total...£ *260*

Received Balance *9th.* day of *Feb* 192*1*.
Geo Hancock

Notice to Third Class (Steerage) Passengers.

1.—If Third Class (Steerage) Passengers, through no default of their own, are not received on board on the day named in their Contract Tickets or fail to obtain a passage in the Ship, they should apply to the Emigration Officer at the Port, who will assist in obtaining redress under the Merchant Shipping Acts.

2.—Third Class (Steerage) Passengers should carefully keep this part of their Contract Ticket till after the end of the Voyage.

N.B.—This Contract Ticket is exempt from Stamp Duty.

[SEE BACK.

The ticket information from the Aberdeen Line booking by James Barry for himself and his family in February 1921.

The Barrys on their new farm in Victoria, Australia, 1921.
courtesy The Barry family, Australia

letters, documents and photographs, many of them collected from relatives living in Ulster and England, were on display.

Among the documents was a letter sent from Loch, on 30 May 1921, to the Templeton family of Ballyedward, Magheramorne, neighbours to the Barrys. In it James Barry writes of the voyage to a new land:

> We had a nice passage, none of us were sick. The decks of the ship were never wet so you may guess we had a splendid passage. We had 1500 passengers aboard, no want of amusement. It was very hot the last four weeks of the passage. We had no trouble getting through whatever. Mr Wilson and a sister Mrs Lawerence met us at Melbourne Harbour. They had house ready for us so that we had no trouble. Mrs Lawerence took Susan and family for a week, which was very nice of her. William got Diphtheria aboard the ship he was in hospital the last three weeks aboard and four weeks in Melbourne Hospital. Mr Wilson got me work with a neighbour farmer at ploughing and sowing . . . I have about 10 acres ploughed and sowed, it's about four inches long now. I have about 10 acres more to plough in the same paddock, but by the time you get this we will be in a home of our own. Its a dairy farm about 200 acres. I have taken it as a going concern, their (sic) is 60 cows, four horses, 30 pigs . . .

The letter continues, providing the information that the Barry family will be living around three miles from Wilson and four miles from the school.

Anna Barry and her brother Wilson mark the 70th anniversary of the family's arrival in Australia. Anna, who never married, died in 1992, and many male children whom she brought into the world as a midwife were given the Christian name Barry in her honour. Wilson left behind an effecting account of the early depression years in Australia when the family could not afford to pay their rent on their farm.
courtesy The Barry family, Australia

The Barrys prospered over the years more than they could have ever hoped at their old home at Magheramorne, County Antrim. James Barry may well have reflected on this as he watched the property and livestock of the family increase in Victoria.

Sadly James would meet an unfortunate end in the land of his adoption, dying from injuries received in a car crash at the age of 76 years in October 1951. Eight people had been injured, five of them seriously, when two vehicles collided. The contemporary Australian newspaper report noted:

> Mr Barry was the younger son of the late William and Sarah Barry, of Magheramorne, County Antrim, Northern Ireland, and had reached the age of 76 years. In 1921, with his wife and family he emigrated to Australia and settled in the Loch district where he took up farming pursuits and in 1924 he purchased the well-known 'Ashton' property originally selected by the late Homer Bros, and was actively associated with this property until the time of his death. . . Of a kindly understanding disposition, Mr Barry befriended and dispensed hospitality to many of his fellow countrymen, a number of whom mingled with the mourners at the funeral on Monday.[78]

Susan Barry died the year following her husband. She had been born at Magheramorne, County Antrim, on 3 July 1876.

The children of the family were headed by Mary, the oldest at 15 years when they emigrated. She trained as a nurse in a Melbourne Hospital and married a local Irishman called Tony Kennedy, their marriage producing four children (three boys and a girl). The eldest boy, John, purchased the property his parents had leased for many years.

Wilson was nine years old when they arrived in Australia. He and his brother William leased a farm at near-by Poowong for a few years and he later purchased his own property in the area and acquired a second farm close by some years later. He married Doris Chaffey and the couple had two boys and two girls; both the sons became farmers, and would later remarry in later life.

William Barry was the second eldest of the children (13 years old when they emigrated). After leasing a property with Wilson for five years from 1930, he purchased 106 acres from his parents and farmed Springfield Farm from 1944–1967. In 1960, at the age of 52, a branch fell on William while working on the farm, leaving him paralysed from the waist down. He retired to Korumburra in 1967 and passed away in 1980. He was married, his wife being Daisy Springfield, and they had six children (five boys and a girl).

Sarah, who was 11 years old when the Barry's went to Australia, trained as a dress maker, working in a department store in Melbourne and later owning her own dress shop in Korumburra. She married a farmer called Alex McKenzie and the couple had two daughters.

The fifth of the Barry children, John, was seven years old when the family arrived. He trained as a schoolteacher and taught at a town close to Loch. He married a local girl, Lorna Slavin, and in his mid-thirties had a career change and became a policeman, being stationed at Ballarat. The couple had four children, two boys and two girls, and John retired and died in Ballarat.

The youngest of the Barry children was James, who was just three when the family emigrated. He lived at Ashton most of his life and in 1944 purchased 100 acres of land from his parents. He married a local girl called Betty Lancey and they had one boy and four girls. James farmed Ashton from 1944 until his death in 1981, and his son Greig and grandson Bill's 800 acres in recent years include the original 255 acres of the Barry holding.

At the Barry Family Reunion at Ashton 68 years after the journey of the family from Larne to Loch, a plaque was unveiled commemorating the arrival of James and Susan and their children in Australia. Seven gum trees, representing each of the seven members of the family, were also planted there, a sign that the legacy of the Barry's of Bankhall would continue in the land of their adoption.[79]

Another exile family, the Alexanders of Ballarat, in the same fertile Victoria landscape which the Barry's settled in, also marked their success with a family gathering in the 1980s. There were 130 descendants of Samuel and Maggie Alexander of Greenland, Larne, and their 15 children, and over half of them attended the event in the town of Learmouth. The family had settled at Bo-peep, near Burrumbeet, a property then still in the possession of the grandson of the early pioneers, Trevor Alexander. The special guest at the May 1987 reunion was Mrs Lottie Holmes, the only surviving member of the 15 children of the Ulster couple.[80] There had been many family gatherings over the years, among them the marriage of the eldest daughter of the Alexanders in 1910. Agnes Jane Alexander was wed to William Herbert Thomas of Ballarat and the couple entertained their families at the Pavilion in the Ballarat Botanical Gardens following the wedding in the Scots Church. Later a large gathering of friends and relatives waved them off from the station as they began a honeymoon taking in Melbourne, Sydney and the Blue Mountains.[81] Interestingly some years ago I heard the story from a local person of how they had been visiting Ballarat and were enjoying a trip to the mining museum there. As they were talking to their wife, one of the attendants approached them and asked if they were from County Antrim, having recognised the accent. The lady had never been to Northern Ireland, but was one of the Alexanders of Ballarat, and it was quite a coincidence that she should meet up with two Larne people that day!

Evidence shows that many others who left smallholdings in Ulster could expect to have large farms in new lands. In areas such as the Canadian provinces and Australia in the 19th and 20th centuries, efforts were made to attract farming stock from 'the old country', just as similar incentives had operated in 18th century South Carolina; in the latter context, for example, there had been land grants of 100 acres for the head of a settler household and 50 for each family member.[82] Given families of six or eight in many cases, the acreage mounted up considerably, as might be imagined. Areas looking for settlers were quick to point to the advantages (needless to say disadvantages were not stressed), as was the case with an 1840 article about New Zealand:

> The surface of the islands is estimated to contain 95,000 square miles, or about sixty million acres being a territory nearly as large as Great Britain; of which, after allowing for mountainous districts and water, it is believed that at least two-thirds are as susceptible of beneficial cultivation. Even without assuming any degree of fertility, New Zealand is thus capable of maintaining as large a population as the British Isles, which, however, it far surpasses in every respect of soil and climate. [83]

Not everyone would have a large area of land grant to call his or her own, but many did. A letter from William Hill in the South Carolina town of Abbeville home to David Hill of Ballynure, County Antrim, in 1855 details that he has bought a house which cost $1250 – a considerable sum, suggesting prosperity – and additionally he also had six Negro slaves valued at $6,000. Hill was, perhaps not surprisingly, considering having his son Robert educated in an Irish college.[84] At an earlier stage, in the 1750s, members of the Houston family from Islandmagee in County Antrim had arrived in Anson and Rowan counties in North Carolina. Archibald Houston was granted some 189 acres in April 1753, this being added to by a further 500 acres land grant in 1764, while David Houston received 495 acres in Anson County around the same period, giving some example of the amounts of land involved in settlement grants at the time.[85] The reminders of many of these settlers in such areas as the Carolinas remain through their descendants, their churches and their cemeteries today. But while the bulk of 18th century settlement from the north of Ireland could be found in America, there are examples of farming settlers elsewhere faring equally as well. Ulsterman Neal Dempsey, who emigrated to New Zealand when he was 18 years old, became a successful farmer and owner of 1,000 acres of land, for example.[86]

Others would also prosper, among them Matthew John Macmillan Robinson, a grazier in New South Wales who was the son of Rev Dr Archibald Robinson, minister of First Broughshane Presbyterian Church for many years. Robinson emigrated to Australia and became a business associate of Sir Samuel McCaughey, the 'Australian Sheep King'. When Robinson died in 1929 he left an estate valued at £210,000 and bequests included one to the Aged and Infirm Ministers Fund of the Presbyterian Church of Ireland.[87]

In 1851 when William Hackett, a native of North Antrim, died, he left his lands in Yorkville, South Carolina, to his brother Hugh at Drumahagles, Ballymoney, and court records in South Carolina show that these were transferred by Hugh to his son William, who had emigrated to live with his uncle two years prior to his death. The Hackett example is an interesting instance of how family networks existed; the deposition of James Adams of Ballywillan in County Antrim related that he was a cousin of the Hacketts. Under oath, he declared that:

> Deponent saith he well recalls the fact and the period of the departure of his cousin William Hackett from this Country for America, which took place in or about the year 1811. Saith Deponent was aware at that time that said William Hackett was then going to reside with his uncle one William Hackett who Deponent heard and believes was then resident in South Carolina in the United States of America, and on this occasion the Deponent conveyed him in company with some others of his family for several miles on his way to Derry at which port he embarked for America and saith said William Hackett never returned to this Country and saith that said William Hackett had only one brother, Hugh Hackett of Drumahagles, and two sisters Mary and Jenny, said that the said Mary died in America upwards of twenty years ago, and that Jenny married one Robert Mallet about the year 1823 and went in the year 1830 or thereabouts with her husband to reside in America where she has ever since resided and as Deponent has heard and believes is now a widow. Saith the said Hugh Hackett's eldest son William Hackett left this country nearly two years ago and went to America to his said uncle William Hackett and is as Deponent believes now residing in Yorkville where his uncle had resided up to the time of his death . . . [88]

The Hackett story outlines how family networks were established and also, one suspects, how the presence of family members across the Atlantic provided a very useful economic outlet. William Hackett, in going out to live with his uncle, was providing family support on the farm and his reward would be the inheritance of several hundred acres of land, houses and buildings.

A similar situation developed with the Lyle family of County Antrim, who emigrated to Timber Ridge, Virginia, in the 18th century and formed a major dynasty connecting to other prominent Ulster emigre families such as the McDowells, also from the same rural district in County Antrim. When Matthew Lyle died in 1774 the terms of his will were that his daughter Elizabeth should receive 110 acres of land on Timber Ridge, conditional that "she come in from Ireland within the term of three years". Elizabeth, who had married at home while her parents emigrated to Virginia, would make the journey from County Antrim with her second husband Matthew Donald and three daughters to her first husband, William Thompson, who had died in 1759, and would set up a new home in accordance with the instructions in her father's will.[89]

Walnut Grove Plantation house was built by Charles and Mary Moore, believed to be from County Antrim, in the 18th century. The family received a land grant from George III which attracted them from their original settlement in Pennsylvania. Walnut Grove, once a successful plantation, is now a museum.

An Australian settler, Sam McCalmont, was the son of a Comber man and was born near Ballynure, County Antrim. He left for Laverton, Western Australia, where he took up ranching with his two brothers John and James. Like many settlers, McCalmont prospered, something which is attested to by the fact that he returned to visit his family and friends after several years in his new home. This visit, in 1910, was to be a poignant one, however, for he died a few years later.[90]

For the early settlers on the land, as for the McCalmont brothers, hundreds of acres of land meant hard work and long hours in preparing the land for productivity. Ballynahinch native Andrew Cloakey, was taken by his parents on a journey to Canada at the age of 14 years. It was noted that in Huron County, Ontario, where the family first settled, they "endured all those hardships and privations associated with early pioneer life". Andrew prospered as a farmer and was described as a man of great vigour, something which can be testified to by the fact that at the age of 80 he moved west and established a new homestead in Alberta. At the age of 90 he was still driving almost 50 miles with a wagon load of produce and at 100 it was said of him that "He possesses all his faculties, and is a living example of what an active life in the Canadian West can do for a man."[91]

While not all would live to such a grand age as Andrew Cloakey, there was little doubt that the Ulster pioneers were a tough breed. The Penny family from Ballycarry emigrated to Canada in 1895, taking with them seven of their eight children. Their grandson, Doug Penny of Calgary, Alberta, recounted that:

> They had purchased unbroken land from the Hudson Bay Company and the Canadian Pacific Railway (CPR) in 1895. The original log and sod house still stands as a part of the addition. The Penny family broke the prairie soil, first with oxen, then to steam engines and later the gasoline and diesel tractor. Horses were always a part of the Canadian scene and served well even after the advent of the tractor. The total land parcel was a half section or 320 acres and this parcel is still in the Penny name, even though it has changed ownership over the years.[92]

The land was close to the town of Abernethy and supplies to it had to be hauled about fifty miles from the railway halt at Indian Head, a two day round trip. It was, said Doug Penny, pioneering in the true sense and conditions were particularly tough in the winters when the temperatures were cold, bitter winds blew and snow drifts were high and dangerous. The payback for hard work came in that the soil was very fertile for wheat, oats and barley, grain and hay which served to feed the livestock. Conditions were improved considerably in the early 1900s when a branch line of the Canadian Pacific was constructed near the farm and passed through Abernethy.

Doug's father Richard was the youngest of the Penny children and was born in 1880. He died in 1968, a day before his 88th birthday. His wife, who had been a Morrison and was Scottish, predeceased her husband in 1961. "They were wonderful parents and did have some difficult times in the early 1930s. They were good Canadians but were always proud of their Irish and Scottish roots," Doug Penny relates.

One Ulster farming family provided Canada with important developments in breed use on farms and methods of preserving green fodder. James C Quinn, the son of Richard Quinn and Jane Cochrane, was born in 1845 and emigrated to Canada in 1873 at the age of 28. He spent time in Newfoundland and Nova Scotia before settling in New Brunswick. As an ordained cleric he would move again, in 1885, to Manitoba, but it was not as a clergyman that he would be best remembered, but for pioneering introduction of a system for preserving green fodder in silos – known as ensilage – in New Brunswick. Quinn also introduced

Doug Penny, whose father was from Windy Gap near Whitehead. Doug returned to Northern Ireland to visit during the Second World War when he was serving in Europe with the Canadian Air Force.

Sam McCalmont, a native of Ballynure, County Antrim, prospered on a farm in Australia after emigrating with his two brothers. He died in 1910.

Shropshire sheep and Ayrshire cattle into the province, proving to be a pioneer of a different kind that those who broke the first soils of the prairie as settlers.[93]

Another settler would be as pioneering in the location in which he settled. John McKee did not invent or adapt anything which proved of a major significance, but his claim to fame lay in his being the first man in Minniehaha County, Sioux Falls, South Dakota in the USA, to make the first set of harnesses. McKee, who was born in the townland of Blackhill near the County Antrim village of Ballycarry in June 1847, learned the trade of a saddler and harness maker at the age of 16 and five years later emigrated to New York. In September 1871 he had made his way to Sioux Falls and it was on the farm of William Bailey that he produced the first set of harnesses in the county. This was the beginning of his commercial success as the following year he opened up a harness shop in the developing town of Sioux Falls. McKee would rise to become a County Commissioner and prominent resident of the area, his trade assisting the farming economy in his new home.[94]

Farming was, as with every occupation in an age of pioneers, dangerous on occasion. The father of future US President Andrew Jackson is said to have died after overworking himself on the land which the family had obtained in the Waxhaw region of South Carolina, and although land grants could be large, their occupation and delivery to a level of production required arduous work. While the death of County Antrim settler Samuel McCloy Stewart in July 1914 was an unusual circumstance, it serves to highlight the potential danger for many. Stewart was a native of Cairncastle, County Antrim, and had been born in 1889. At the age of 15 years he went with his sister to Virden in Manitoba, where her husband and another brother had begun farming the year previously. Around 1906 the Stewarts and Duffins would move to Central Butte, Saskatchewan, and in December 1912 Stewart married Catherine McArthur, whose family had come to the area from Ontario. Sadly it was to be a short marriage, for on a July day the following year a lightning storm blew up when Sam Stewart was working at the farm of a neighbour. As they tried to get the team of horses to a barn, lightning struck the 25-year-old and he died instantly, leaving behind his wife and their young daughter Agnes Jean. It was noted in an obituary that among those mourning their loss were his two brothers in New Zealand and two brothers and two sisters living with his parents at Cairncastle, County Antrim.[95]

For many families, however, life on the land, while it could be severe, was not as cruel. And for small tenant farmers or landowners in Ulster the pull must have been a great one when they opened weekly newspapers to find adverts encouraging them to emigrate to different parts of the British Empire. In March 1903, for example, one such advertisement offered 160 acre farms in Western Canada under the slogan "Free Farms! No More Rent for Farmers!" and informing readers that a delegation of Canadian farmers was visiting Ulster:

> Any person desiring to meet and consult the Delegates with a view to securing information about Canada drawn from their personal experiences as practical and successful agriculturalists are invited to send their names and addresses without delay to Mr Edward O'Kelly, Canadian Government Agent, 13 Queen's Square, Belfast.[96]

An entire series of articles appeared in one provincial newspaper's weekly columns in 1908, outlining the virtues of life in each section of Canada and being sure to mention local people to be found there. One example was from Alberta, which outlined what life was like and what prospects awaited in Edmonton and the Peace River district. Farmers would have been encouraged to read that the country surrounding Edmonton was said to be the most fertile in the North West of Canada. "The Future of Edmonton is assured. Any town with its record deserves to prosper," the article stated,[97] adding that Edmonton was seen as a gateway to the rich lands beyond – ". . . a land of promise, awaiting a populace to whom it offers with assurance prospects seldom met with elsewhere." In order to further encourage the would-be settler, there were extensive advertising campaigns and visits from delegations and speakers sent to entice emigrants. For many,

it was hard to resist the opportunities which were promised.

The epitome of what could be achieved in new lands of opportunity was provided by Sir Samuel McCaughey, who was known as Australia's Sheep King. He was born at Tullynewey near Ballymena in the 1830s and emigrated to Australia in 1856 as a young man in his 20s to work as a labourer.[98] He started his emigrant life in Australia as a 'jackeroo' – or apprentice – at his uncle's sheep station in Victoria, becoming manager within two years. In 1860 McCaughey bought a station in New South Wales with two partners and built up a famous stud.

His flair for agriculture and business was highlighted by his acquisition of other stations and his introduction of irrigation methods and investment in improving yield and quality of wool. At one stage his stations were shearing a million sheep a year and Samuel McCaughey became the wealthiest man in the state. He also rose to prominent in the social and political arena, being a Member of the Legislative Council between 1899 and his death in 1919. Knighted in 1905, he was a strong supporter of Ulster Unionists during the Home Rule period, while his patriotism for his adopted homeland was highlighted by his presentation of twenty warplanes to the government in the First World War. Something of a measure of his commercial success is that fact that he bequeathed nearly £2,000,000 for education and charitable purposes when he died, unmarried, at North Yanco, New South Wales, on 25 July 1919.[99] His former home there was bought by the state and is now the Yanco Agricultural High School, a fitting remembrance of an Ulster emigrant who had also an inventive bent; McCaughey invented some useful farm implements – the double furrow plough which was capable of loosening the subsoil, and an earth scoop, called 'Tumbling Tommy' which reduced the cost of tank sinking on the sheep stations by 60 to 70 per cent.

Another Ulstermen of inventive bent was Robert Dalzell, son of a leader in the 1798 Rebellion. He was born near Belfast in 1793 and would win fame in the United States, where he became inventor of the grain elevator.[100] The inventor of the farm reaper, Cyrus McCormick, was also, of course, of Ulster stock.

Not everyone, of course, could be a Samuel McCaughey, a Robert Dalzell or a Cyrus McCormick. But the prospect of plentiful land brought with it the opportunity for many of economic betterment. There were some who did not succeed, but there were many more who did; the words of James Houston, writing home to his mother in Larne in 1836 from Louisiana in the United States echoed many similar messages; "Money is very plenty and nobody thinks of saving but all of making it."[101]

Many of Ulster's emigrants were rurally based and settled on the land as farmers or operated in an agriculturally-based economy. Country stores such as that of the Ulster-Scot McGills in York County, South Carolina, were an integral part of life in rural areas.

74   Information from the Barry family, Loch, Victoria
75   Letter from James Barry to his neighbour, Mr Templeton of Magheramorne, May 21, 1921
76   Typescript of Wilson Barry's memories from the Barry family, Loch, Victoria
77   *South Gippsland Sentinel Times*, 16 June 1992
78   'James Barry's Farewell. The story of a local emigrant family and a new life in Australia' by Dr David Hume in the *Broadisland Journal*, Vol Two, Ballycarry, County Antrim, 1996
79   See Dr D Hume, James Barry's Farewell: the story of a local emigrant family and a new life in Australia, *Broadisland Journal*, Volume 2, 1996
80   *The Courier*, Ballarat, Victoria, 27 May 1987
81   *Larne Times*, April 30, 1910, from the *Ballarat Star*
82   Walter Edgar, *South Carolina. A History*, University of South Carolina Press, Columbia, 1998
83   *Belfast News Letter*, 1 December 1840
84   Letter from William Hill, Abbeville, South Carolina, 24 January 1855, held by the Public Record Office of Northern Ireland
85   Papers of the late WC Houston of Philadelphia, copy in the Public Record Office of Northern Ireland, T.342
86   *Weekly Telegraph*, 10 January 1931
87   *Weekly Telegraph*, 3 August 1929
88   York County, South Carolina, deed book Q, p254, in the archives of the York County Historical Commission
89   Oscar K Lyle, Lyle Family. *The Ancestry and Posterity of Matthew, John, Daniel and Samuel Lyle, Pioneer Settlers in Virginia*, New York, 1912
90   *Larne Times*, 19 April 1913
91   *Northern Whig*, 6 December 1923
92   Memoir of Doug Penny, Calgary, Alberta, August 1996
93   *East Antrim Times*, 4 March 1971
94   *Larne Times* and *Weekly Telegraph*, 28 June 1913
95   *Larne Times*, 8 August 1914
96   *Weekly Telegraph*, 7 March 1903
97   This quotation is from one of a series of articles in the *Weekly Telegraph* on Canada in 1908, all extolling the potential of the area to would-be emigrants.
98   *News Letter*, 11 January 1988
99   *A Dictionary of Irish Biography*, Henry Boylan (ed.), Gill & Macmillan, Dublin, 1998.
100 *Appleton's Cyclopedia of American Biography*
101 Letter from James Houston to his mother, 8 March 1836, Public Record Office of Northern Ireland.

Canny in commerce: Ulster folk in business and employment overseas

Emigrants who left our shores embarked on a wide variety of occupations and employment in their new homes. Some would become highly prominent in their chosen fields, others would not. Some would amass a fortune and, indeed, lose it. Others would live comfortably and some would not live so well at all; the father of President Andrew Johnson, for example, was as poor when he died shortly after a brave rescue of three men whose boat had overturned on a city pond in the January of 1812 in Raleigh, North Carolina, as when his family had emigrated from County Antrim.[102]

When it comes to Ulster exiles doing well – commerce being one example – few names surpass that of Timothy Eaton, a County Antrim emigrant whose business empire made him one of the most famous men in Canada. Eatons Stores was an almost certain place for Ulstermen and women to find employment (particularly, some said, if they were Protestant), if they were prepared to work. The Eaton Empire owed much to the young Timothy's apprenticeship to a relative who ran a general store in Portglenone, where the future businessman had to sleep under a counter of the store on occasions because he had to open up at 4am on market days. William Smith, who ran the business, stocked dry goods, hardware, feeds, liquor and other items, and it was said that it was where Timothy Eaton came to nurse an implacable hatred of class distinctions based on wealth[103].

He was born at Clogher townland near Ballymena shortly after the death of his father, John Eaton. The ninth child of the family, his mother Margaret (Craig) Eaton named him after her late husband's favourite book of the Bible. Timothy, when he was old enough, was sent to Ballymena Academy, but his experience there was not a happy one; he was picked on by the town boys because of his homespun clothes. He remained none too impressed with the idea of secondary education into later life, probably due to his experiences at 'the Academy'.

The conditions were clearly right for Timothy Eaton to consider a life elsewhere by the time he had found how difficult working for William Smith in Portglenone was. His brother Robert had emigrated to Canada when he was 24 years old, and a family network was established which offered the Eatons the possibility of betterment across the Atlantic. Thus it was that in 1854 Timothy took ship, moving to Canada in the footsteps of his older brother. He obtained a job in a store at the village of Glen Williams, followed by another at a village called Kirkton. His brother James had also come to Canada, meanwhile, and in 1860 the pair opened up a store – J&T Eaton's – at a town called St Marys, offering dry goods, groceries, boots and shoes, hardware and patent medicines. These fledgling attempts were to bear much greater fruit as time went on.

In 1862 he married and seven years later he and his wife Maggie moved to Toronto, where Timothy would found the first Eaton's store, offering quality goods for cash only and at one low price for everyone. The store expanded, with branches being opened elsewhere across Canada, and it was obvious that Eaton's sound business ideas had struck the right chord with the buying public. When Timothy Eaton died in 1907 his empire was such that his company employed 2,500 staff and operated not only in towns and cities across Canada but also by mail order. In the 1960s his business successors employed 40,000 people.

That Eaton's readily offered employment to emigrants from Ulster is highlighted in just one newspaper account from 1929. It was noted that Charles Davison, formerly of Larne, had been appointed manager of the new store in the flourishing town of Moose Jaw, Saskatchewan. An ex-serviceman – something which also carried a high degree of respect within the Eaton empire – he had served with the Royal Irish Fusiliers in the Balkans and later in Palestine during the First World War. His promotion came after being a buyer for two years for the Winnipeg store of T Eaton and Company.[104]

Millionaire as he was, Timothy Eaton was not the only business magnet from Ulster in Canada. The founder of the Dominion Stores was a native of Gilford in County Down called WJ Pentland, and in the 1930s his stores employed over 3,000, many of them also Ulster exiles like himself. Pentland had obtained early business training in the offices of the Belfast Ropeworks Ltd, and in 1911 emigrated to the United States, where he was, for eight years, superintendent of the Atlantic and Pacific Tea Company, which had over 17,000 stores. The experienced gained there led to his founding of the Dominion Stores in Canada. Sadly Pentland was killed in an accident at the age of 45 years in 1933.[105]

In New Zealand the name of the Entrican Brothers was well known in Auckland business circles. The firm of Entrican and Company once stood at Customs Street in Auckland, in a building which highlighted their Ulster origins. Tyrone Buildings was the headquarters of the general merchants premises, and the two brothers who founded it were both significant civic and commercial figures in the New Zealand of the late 19th and early 20th centuries.

The business was founded by Andrew Jack Entrican in 1887 and he was joined in business by his brother James Cuthbertson Entrican about five years later.

They were sons of Robert Entrican, a farmer from Craigmonaghan House, Castlederg, County Tyrone. Andrew was educated at school in Castlederg and started work with a general merchant in Londonderry called Andrew Rosborough in 1874. In 1880 he emigrated to New Zealand, landing at Auckland from the ship *Ben Nevis*, and became a retail grocer and commercial traveller for some years before establishing his own business. James was born near Sion, County Tyrone, in 1864 and was also educated at Edwards National School, Castlederg. He became an apprentice to a Liverpool merchant after leaving school and after completing his apprenticeship determined to head to the Colonies, arriving in New Zealand in 1885 on the SS *Tongariro*.

Soon afterwards James entered into partnership with a man named RW Gallaugher, who traded under the name Gallaugher and Entrican, grocers and Italian warehousemen, on Victoria Street West, Auckland.

After about seven years the Tyrone man retired from the firm and joined his brother.

The two brothers were active in more than the commercial life of Auckland, for they also became civic leaders. James served on the local Borough Council for the Devonport and also Mount Albert areas, while Andrew was an Auckland City Council member.

James was a member of the Auckland Museum council and donated a collection of coins and medals to a local museum in the city – appropriately enough, in the circumstances, titled the Old Colonists Museum. He was associated with the co-operative movement in the city, and also the Presbyterian Church, being a Sunday School teacher at the Devonport Presbyterian congregation and a member of the Kirk session.

Andrew Entrican was regarded as the 'father' of the city council and was deputy mayor for Auckland for many years. He was also a former chairman and long-term member of the Auckland Harbour Board, and his other civic involvements included the Auckland Fire Board, Auckland Savings Bank, Auckland Chamber of Commerce and Auckland Merchant's Association. His service on the city council was divided into three periods: 1898–1901, 1903–1920 and 1923–1935.

Like his brother, Andrew was also active in the Presbyterian Church, and was an elder in St James' congregation in Wellington Street in the city and also involved with the Sunday School as superintendent for some 47 years. One of his former pupils was a future mayor of Auckland named Baildon, under whom Entrican would later serve as deputy mayor.

Both men were involved in many civic organisations and were familiar and highly respected figures in their Auckland of their era.

James and Andrew Entrican, Ulster businessmen in Auckland, New Zealand. The pair named their store in the city the Tyrone Buildings.
Photos courtesy of Fairfax Newspapers, New Zealand.

The city changed considerably in their lifetimes, and in his memoirs Andrew Entrican recalled how he had sailed into Auckland harbour on a Sunday morning in 1880. He remembered that the church bells were ringing; "I thought it was God's own country, and I think so still", he told a gathering after his retirement from the city council in 1935.

An article in the *New Zealand Observer* of 5 March 1936, provides an interesting anecdote about the Tyrone man, outlining that he was a strong supporter of temperance. But, said the *Observer*:

> He was also a North of Ireland man with strong sentiment for his native land and people, and on a visit to the Auckland Hospital to see an old and unfortunate Ulsterman, he asked the patient if there was anything he could do to make his lot easier. The Irishman replied that the only thing he really wanted was some Guinness's stout, so Mr Entrican went straight out, crossed the Grafton Bridge to the Caledonian Hotel, and bought two bottles that he took back to his ailing compatriot. This was said to be the only occasion on which the late AJ Entrican entered a public bar.

Andrew Jack Entrican died in his 87th year, on 19 February 1936, at his home on Remuera Road, Auckland, being survived by his wife Elizabeth Mary (nee Mackay, eldest daughter of a prominent ship-owner and builder) and son RG Entrican. The Auckland businessman, whose last resting place was at Waikaraka cemetery in the city, was described in one newspaper account as a man who had "an unsurpassed record of service to local government, extending over 38 years" while "his work for public causes of all kinds covered nearly half a century".

"Mr Entrican will be remembered among those who have rendered most distinguished services to the city of Auckland", another newspaper reflected.

Andrew was survived by his younger brother James until the 1950s. He died at the age of 86 in March 1951 and was survived by his wife and a daughter, Mrs J Baird of Christchurch.

That both men remembered their Ulster origins was not only clear from the name of their premises – Tyrone Buildings – but also from the fact that Jack was prominent in the Auckland Ulster Association which once thrived in the city. When the Association held a memorial service in St James' Presbyterian Church in honour of him, it was attended by members of the City Council and a large gathering of friends and acquaintances, underlining the strong Ulster community that existed there and the connections which its members had in the wider city social circle.[106]

Some businessmen were pioneers in their own right in terms of settlement as well. One such, for example, was James Darragh of Ballymena, who was one of the oldest residents and most successful businessmen of the Thames district of Auckland, New Zealand, where he died in 1903[107]. It was

noted that he had been born in 1840 and arrived in Victoria, Australia, in 1858, being lured there by the goldfields. He remained there for around four years before moving to New Zealand, where he enjoyed success at gold rushes there too. His new found wealth was used to establish a business as a carter. His understandable interest remained in the goldfields, however, and this brought him to the Thames district in 1867. He developed an interest in the lumber trade, particularly in railway sleeper provision, and had large business interests at the time of his death in 1903.

Another common factor which Darragh had with many other Ulster emigrants was the large size of their families; the Ballymena man was survived by seven sons and two daughters.

Another emigrant regarded as a pioneer was Nicholas McAlpine, a native of Comber in County Down. McAlpine had a varied business career, which started with a grist and saw mill, then saw him involved in banking and finally in railroad building. He was born in County Down in April 1835 and emigrated to Pittsburgh at the age of 17, staying there for a few years before travelling to live with his uncle John McAlpine, one of the founders of the city of Kansas (then called Wyandott). In 1866 he was elected to civic office, holding the post of city treasurer. At the age of 65, when most men would be considering a healthy retirement and less exertion, Nicholas McAlpine headed to Colorado to commence a new portfolio in mining operations, and would later travel to Alaska for the same purpose. He died in 1908, being survived by three of a family and a number of relatives in his native land. An obituary noted:

> Mr McAlpine was a man of remarkable business attainments and good executive ability. He accumulated two very respectable sized fortunes, and prior to the financial crisis of 1893 was worth from a quarter to half a million dollars, but depreciation of values coupled with numerous endorsements, practically eat his resources up. He was public-spirited, imbued with great energy and perseverance, honest and upright in his dealings, charitably inclined and always ready to extend a helping hand to the needy and unfortunate, a good citizen and a reliable and loyal friend.[108]

The idea of 'the American Dream' was something that drove many emigrants forward, the belief that in the United States all things were possible. Although some such as Nicholas McAlpine could amass a small fortune and then lose it through the vagaries of the economic market, this would not have been a common story. And the realisation of 'the American Dream' made it possible for Belfast man Samuel McClean to become President of one of the biggest firms in the packing industry in the United States at the age of just 35 years. He was also director of many other business concerns. Yet a quarter of a century before, McClean had entered the employ of the Anglo-American Packing Company as a messenger boy. He would rise to President of its successor, the

Northern Packing Company, Chicago, and was also a director of Continental Packing, Omaha Packing, Anglo-American Provision Company, Fowler Packing, National Car Line Company and others – a highly impressive list.[109]

An earlier Ulster figure was John Gordon McComb, who emigrated with his wife and family from the rural district of Dunturkey near Ballynure, County Antrim, to the New World. John McComb settled in Albany, New York, and set up a provision business, having as a lucrative market the army officers based nearby, who bought up luxury goods, wines, books and snuff. His son Alexander followed in his father's footsteps and earned a fortune trading with the Indian communities as well as local townspeople. His business was so profitable that he was able to invest £100,000 in New York, a considerable fortune in the pre-Revolutionary years.

The McCombs were unlike many of the Presbyterian settlers in America in that they remained loyal to the Crown when the Revolution broke out, but given their involvement and extensive business interests with the military this was probably hardly surprising; John McComb raised a militia of 500 men to support the Crown forces, showing clearly where his sympathies lay. His son was also loyal to the Crown but after the War of Independence he pledged his loyalty to the new American state. His brother William continued to live and trade through Canada, but Alexander would return to New York. There was something of an irony in the fact that Alexander's impressive home in Broadway, New York, was leased for a time to the American President, George Washington.

Alexander McComb became a business tycoon, having 25 servants including 12 slaves to look after himself and his family, and acquiring four and a half million acres of land. Unfortunately the fate of Comber's John McAlpine also became McComb's lot, for speculation in shares brought financial disaster and he became bankrupt and had to be saved from a debtor's prison by his friend, Alexander Hamilton. His son, also named Alexander, would make a more lasting contribution as General McComb, who gained victory in the War of 1812 – which also brought another Ulster-Scot, Andrew Jackson, to national fame and prominence. McComb was awarded a gold medal by Congress and promoted to Major General; he would later be Commander in Chief of the American Army until his death in 1841.[110]

The success of some in business and commerce was on a much smaller scale than McComb, McClean or McAlpine, but many emigrants did do well enough for themselves and their families. James K Taylor, a native of Belfast, built up a successful business as a florist and seedsman in his new home in Natal, South Africa, and then Salisbury, Rhodesia[111], while also in Salisbury former Carrickfergus man Charles Holmes was owner of a flourishing pharmacy as well as being Vice-President of the Pharmaceutical Society of Southern Rhodesia and secretary of the Salisbury Chemists Association.[112]

Robert F Craig of Brockville, Ontario, was head of a large department store in the 1960s and combined success in commerce with an interest in his ancestry, having written to a local newspaper in search of information about his grandfather Robert Craig of Carneal, Larne, and grandmother Ellen McKeown of Moy, County Tyrone.[113] W Warren Barbour, who was president of the Linen Thread Company of New Jersey in the USA in the 1920s, was the son of Colonel William Barbour of Lisburn. He traced his commercial and ancestral roots back to John Barbour of Paisley in Scotland, who had moved to Ulster in 1784 and established linen mills near Lisburn, which were later located at Hilden. In 1923 Barbour, whose company had mills in New Jersey, New York, Massachusetts, Maine, Maryland and Alabama, was elected Mayor of Rumson, New Jersey. It was reported that "Although only thirty-five years of age, Mr Barbour has attained a prominence in the business world reached by few."[114]

For at least some of the emigrants, the old adage that it was an ill wind that blew no good was highly appropriate. Thomas Humphreys, for example, was one of those who helped to rebuild Chicago after the major fire in the city in 1871, having gone to the city at an early age to join his brothers, who had a building firm there[115], while another Ulsterman who helped do much to create development was William Calwell, a native of Windy Gap near Whitehead. He emigrated to San Mateo,

W Warren Barbour was the son of a Lisburn man, Colonel William Barbour, and traced his commercial and ancestral roots back to John Barbour of Paisley, Scotland, who moved to Ulster in 1784 and founded linen mills near Lisburn.
Larne Times and Weekly Telegraph, 8 December 1923

California, where his Wisnom relatives had a building firm. The family firm managed to build much of the town, and William Calwell – like Thomas Humphreys – later returned home, bringing design ideas for buildings which included the Bentra Golf Club house at Whitehead and also his own property, The Bungalow, in Ballycarry. An entire row of San Francisco type basement bungalows can also be found in the latter village, a unique reminder of an American influence on an exile who returned to his native land.[116] Robert Wisnom, who had settled in San Mateo after a time in New Zealand, was regarded as founder of the city, and spent fifty years in California, many of the houses in the town being built by the Wisnoms and Calwell.[117]

The Girvan family were well-known builders in their home town of Larne, and when David Girvan emigrated to Sydney, he and his brother carried on the business they had learned from their father Hugh at home in County Antrim,[118] while Hugh Jamison, who was from Belfast, was well-known as a contractor in Johannesburg, South Africa, until his death in 1924.[119] Michael Hawkins of Bangor, County Down, meanwhile, had a varied career which started as an apprentice to a builder in County Down. He emigrated at age 19 to America, with, it was said, only a few shillings, and worked there as a bricklayer before coming home again. In 1884 his desire to seek a new life elsewhere led him to

an emigrant ship which sailed for New Zealand, and here he was more successful, being appointed as a warder and instructor in building at Mount Cook Prison in Wellington. By 1914 he was Director of Prisons and in 1924 became Controller General of Inspectors, retiring two years later. His retirement was taken up, however, by somewhat of a return to his roots, for he became director of the New Era Brick Company, Waitakire.[120]

Joseph Hill, meanwhile, who settled in British Honduras in 1872, would be engaged in the provision of quality woods to Europe, some of which no doubt ended up in the building industry. Born at Larne in June 1799, he emigrated with his father James and mother Rebecca to North Carolina when he was a child. In 1820 he and his father went south to Belize to engage in the trade for hardwoods, mahogany and other woods from the extensive forests. No doubt the climate and the work was hard on the Antrim father and son, but it was possible for them to earn up to 100 gold pieces in one week, Hill recounted in a copy of a letter which ended up in the Crown Colony archives in Belize.[121] The men cut and fetched wood for a merchant in Liverpool, and in later years Joseph Hill would become a builder in the town of Orange Walk, an army barracks being among his constructions. His letter was sent to John Bennett of Knockbreda in Belfast and addressed the issue of his son coming out to the British colony:

A house in San Mateo, California, which was the work of the County Antrim Wisnom firm. The Wisnoms, from the Whitehead area, are regarded as among the founders of San Mateo.

William Calwell, who was a relative of the Wisnom family, emigrated to California and worked for their building firm for several years. He returned home, however, bringing with him ideas for unique architecture. In the village of Ballycarry a row of San Francisco style basement-bungalows were built, along with The Bungalow, Calwell's home on the Main Street, which was erected in 1909 and used timber shingles, a highly uncommon feature for the era.

> If your son Gilbert decides to come here to me he could do well, but cousin, this is a hot land and work is hard now. A man cannot come to any wealth here without sweat and hard labour.

The climate was little different further south, where, in Demerara, fortunes could be made on the sugar plantations. Charles McGarel, who was a major sugar plantation owner in British Guiana and elsewhere in the West Indies, bestowed some of the wealth he made on his native town by way of a town hall, cemetery, and houses for gentlefolk who had fallen on hard times. The most lasting tribute to McGarel's benevolence and his economic position can be seen in the McGarel Town Hall, which graces the corner of Larne's Main Street – it is not an exaggeration to say that its foundations were built on sugar.[122] When McGarel died in 1876 he is believed to have left £600,000 in his will, a vast amount by modern standards, and his properties in County Antrim passed to his brother-in-law, who later became the first Lord Magheramorne.

In 1877 the family connection with Demerara was emphasised in a newspaper report in the *Georgetown Colonist*, which related that a public banquet had been held in honour of Quinton Hogg,[123] brother of Sir James McGarel Hogg. It is clear from the report of the banquet that Hogg had invested heavily in the colony at a time of financial depression. It had obviously been a risk – and the examples of Alexander McComb and Nicholas McAlpine show the negative impact of such investments – but one which had paid off for Hogg and Demerara. His investments had come through purchase and improvement of sugar estates, construction of docks and warehouses and establishment of a direct line of steamers between the colony and Barbados and the ports of London and Glasgow.[124]

Hogg was simply following in the path of his older brother Charles McGarel, who had, in the first quarter of the same century, done much to develop Demerara. In his speech at the banquet Hogg noted of his brother that "as a colonist he was a credit to the colony and as an accumulator of wealth he was a benefactor to the world". Something of the significance which was attached to his own contribution was the fact that it was said that the banquet was attended by the elite of the colony and that almost nine columns of newsprint were devoted to the speeches. It is clear that several men were attracted to the colony from McGarel's home town. In one of the churches in Larne is a memorial plaque to William Johnston, one of those who left a bequest when he died at Demerara at the early age of 43 years, while in St Cedma's burying ground is a large and imposing gravestone, complete with railings, recalling a member of the Kirkpatrick family who also died in the colony. Alexander Barr, who died in the colony in 1894, had been manager at the lime quarries owned by the McGarels at Magheramorne near Larne, prior to emigrating to British Guiana, where he would serve in the colonial legislature and play an important role in the sugar industry. Married to a Creole lady, he had four children and the climate had obviously taken its toll on him; six months before his death he returned to Ulster, to stay in Rostrevor, in an attempt to regain his health.[125] Barr's example illustrates that not all of those who went to Demerara would enjoy success or long life. William McGarel, son of Charles, died at the age of 21 years in the colony on 23 February 1810,[126] his premature death being lamented greatly by his circle of friends.

Evidence that Ulstermen made shrewd business people could be more than adequately gleaned from the story of the Fullertons of Raloo, County Antrim, who established a highly successful lumber company in Louisiana, in the United States, which extended further west into Minneapolis. Thomas Fullerton founded the firm in 1882, along with TM Wallace,

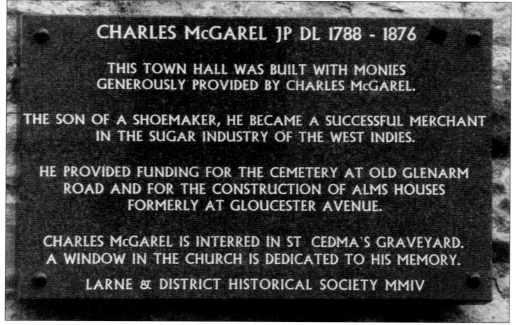

CHARLES McGAREL JP DL 1788 - 1876

THIS TOWN HALL WAS BUILT WITH MONIES GENEROUSLY PROVIDED BY CHARLES McGAREL.

THE SON OF A SHOEMAKER, HE BECAME A SUCCESSFUL MERCHANT IN THE SUGAR INDUSTRY OF THE WEST INDIES.

HE PROVIDED FUNDING FOR THE CEMETERY AT OLD GLENARM ROAD AND FOR THE CONSTRUCTION OF ALMS HOUSES FORMERLY AT GLOUCESTER AVENUE.

CHARLES McGAREL IS INTERRED IN ST CEDMA'S GRAVEYARD. A WINDOW IN THE CHURCH IS DEDICATED TO HIS MEMORY.

LARNE & DISTRICT HISTORICAL SOCIETY MMIV

Above: The McGarel Town Hall in Larne was built as a gift to the town by Charles McGarel, the son of a shoemaker, who made his fortune in sugar plantations in Demerara, and shrewd stock market operations. McGarel also gave the town alms houses, and a cemetery. He is buried at St Cedma's Church in the town.

Left: A plaque to Charles McGarel on the Town Hall which he donated to the town of Larne, and which was erected in 2004 by the town's Historical Society.

A bust of McGarel was presented to Larne following his death by his widow and is located inside the McGarel Town Hall.
by kind permission of Larne Borough Council

John Donelan, a Belfast man who died attempting to save two men who were victims of gas poisoning in 1948. He had been from the Oldpark area of the city and had emigrated to Toronto.

who was President in the 1930s when the company merged with the Midland Lumber and Coal Company, bringing together two of the pioneer lumber distributors in the northwest of the USA. That the Fullertons kept a strong Ulster emphasis in their firm was underlined by the fact that Wallace was a native of Kilwaughter parish in County Antrim, just a few miles from their own home in Raloo.[127]

In the early 19th century the climate of many of the areas in which they settled, and propensity of diseases such as malaria, cholera and others, were too much for many emigrants to contend with. There are also accounts of emigrants dying on the long passages across from these shores to America. As time went on, however, the immune systems became hardened to diseases encountered in their new homes, and deaths became fewer. The saddest tale of emigration

from Ireland generally is that of the 'coffin ships' during the years of the Irish Potato Famine, when disease claimed hundreds of thousands of lives either at sea or on arrival at destinations such as Quebec[128]. The *New York Express* reported in June 1847, for example, that typhoid had claimed numbers on ships which had arrived in Quebec from Londonderry, Belfast and Newry among other ports, and, it was added, "the probability is that the number will augment daily" – something which was sadly true.[129] Most emigrants from Ulster were, thankfully, not prompted to leave by famine and disease, but there are still some accounts of the premature death of exiles abroad.

One such was John Donelan, who left Oldpark in Belfast for a new life in Toronto, where he became a bus driver. A World War two serviceman in the Toronto Irish, he died in a valiant attempt to rescue two men trapped down a well near his home, succumbing to gas poisoning.[130] In 1912 relatives of Henry Morley, a native of Magheraleggan near Downpatrick, were informed of his death in a silver mine in Montana in the United States. Morley had served an apprenticeship in a grocery and spirit business in Downpatrick, before being encouraged to emigrate by his cousin Patrick J Killen – but in a twist of fate Killen was to die in an accident at the smelting works at Grand Forks, British Columbia, about three years before. [131] It would be true to say, however, that certain occupations such as mining and heavy engineering carried with them greater risks than some. Among those in a high risk category would also be firemen, and in 1904 a Ballygawley

Ballygawley man Richard Donnelly , who died in the line of duty as
a fireman in 1904 in New York.

native would lose his life in the course of his duty as a fire-
fighter. Richard Donnelly died from injuries received at the
Kieper Brothers fire, leaving his parents John and Mary to
mourn their loss at home in Tyrone.[132]

On the other hand, there were those who lived into ripe old
age, such as former railroad superintendent Thomas Sloan of
Gutherie, Oklahoma. He was believed to be the oldest person
in the United States when he died in his 116th year in 1928;
he was a native of the Mourne district of County Down.[133]

Robert Johnston, who died at the age of 83 years in 1912,
was a familiar figure in Toronto, where he had followed the
occupation of tailor. Born in Paisley in Scotland to a family
of 12 from Lisburn, he was brought up in the latter town and
lived in Belfast at the time of emigrating to Canada.[134]

The occupations which Ulster emigrants followed were
varied. Jane Kirkwood, for example, trained as a nurse in
Belfast, then graduated in pharmacy from Queens University
before she emigrated to the Dominion of Canada with
her husband William Douds and family in 1928. She died
in 1952.[135] Belfastman John Canning found a new life in
Minneapolis, Minnesota, as a compositor and proofreader,[136]
while James Elliott, who was born in Armagh in 1847, owned
a footwear shop in the town of Maldon in Australia having

started his career as a boot store salesman.[137] James Robinson,
who was born in Larne in 1862, was a pioneer farmer in
Saskatchewan in Canada before becoming a rancher and
in time a road inspector in Medicine Hat, Alberta, while a
newspaper report on County Antrim exile, David Girvan,
who lived near Sydney, New South Wales, detailed in 1926
that he had been appointed a Justice of the Peace, and that
his brother was following a Ulster family tradition of being a
builder and contractor in Artarmon, Sydney.[138]

It was often, however, those who had attained higher socio-
economic status who were mentioned to greater extent in local
newspapers back home in Northern Ireland, among them
John E Boddie, a native of Coleraine, County Londonderry,
who was chief engineer of the Canadian Fish and Cold Storage
Company at Prince Rupert, British Columbia, for some 43
years and whose relatives at home in the UK included his
brother Rear Admiral Boddie, RN, who was prominent in
the Allied attack on Zeebrugge during the First World War.[139]
George Finlay from Londonderry was a dentist and served
in the First World War with the Australian Dental Corps; he
later became Honorary Treasurer of the Australian Dental
Association in the late 1930s.[140] Alexander Sayers, from a
prominent Ballymena and Carnlough, County Antrim, family,
was owner of a successful chemist's business in Wingrove,
Melbourne, and in the Second World War had served as
a sergeant in the Army Medical Corps of the Australian
Expeditionary Force in Egypt and France.[141] Dr Shuldan
Henry Dunlap of North Williamson, Victoria, took his
degrees in medicine in Belfast before emigrating to Australia
to set up a successful practice as a medical practitioner.[142]

There were numerous others who achieved prominence
in their business and professional lives and also, as a
consequence, in public life. William Speers, a native of Larne
and a former member of the Royal Irish Constabulary, retired
from a service career as Commissioner of Police in Kedah,
Malaysia[143], while William Craig of Slatt, Ballymena, became
an Assistant United States District Attorney and a respected
member of the Memphis Bar, while another Ballymena
native, Dr James Houston, was reporter in the Senate of the
United States in 1847 and was reputedly earning $18,000
per Congress for providing Washington newspapers with
reports of debates.[144] John Sayers, who was born in the coastal
village of Carnlough, County Antrim, in 1835, became
one of the most prominent men in Melbourne in the latter
years of the 19th century and was city accountant for the
municipality of South Melbourne.[145] Stewart's Hotel in Larne
was the venue in October 1839 for a farewell supper to a
schoolteacher about to embark for a new life and an extension
of his career, also in Australia. John Kane had been teacher of
the first classical and mercantile school in the town, and the
planned departure was marked by a gathering of many of the
important gentlemen of the town.[146]

Although Australia, Canada and the United States would draw many of the emigrants from Ulster, locals were also to be found in other areas, particularly parts of the British Empire. Francis Dill, for example, was from Donaghmore in County Tyrone, and was Colonial Hospital Surgeon at Hong Kong in the 1840s. He was also founder of the China Medico-Chirurgical Society, but sadly his career and his life were cut short at the early age of 29 years, when he fell victim to a fever.[147] The climate of India must have taken time for William Jenkins to become accustomed to, but in the 1940s medical advances were of great assistance to those travelling to far-off climes. Jenkins, who was from Belfast, worked in insurance, and had taken up a position with Brady & Co Ltd, described as one of the largest firms in India in 1930. Fifteen years later his career was described as 'meteoric' and he was director of the insurance firm as well as a printers, a hotel in Bombay, a large sugar factory and a financial journal. The Belfast man, who had picked up something of around 200 Indian dialects, had also the distinction of being afforded an interview with Mahatma Ghandi.[148]

Among those who made their way to South Africa was James Stewart, a native of the townland of Ballyrickard near Larne. Like hundreds of others, he was drawn to South Africa through militia and yeomanry units who went to fight against the Boers in the South African War. Stewart, however, decided to stay, and worked in the mining industry. However the work led to his being laid off with phthisis (pulmonary tuberculosis) and eventually brought about his death at the age of 42 years. It was reported that he was laid to rest in Boksburg, following a service in the Roman Catholic Church there.[149]

It did not matter, of course, what equipment one had if one did not strike it lucky at 'the diggings', as Carrickfergus exile Noah Dalway found out in the 1850s when he headed off to Forest Creek beyond Melbourne. He was reduced to being able to afford food for only one meal a day at one stage, eventually finding enough gold at another 'field' to earn him £25 by the end of sixteen months. In 1857 he had invested his savings of £40 in quartz mining, a business venture which failed, and he later was fortunate to find a fellow Carrickfergus man named William Reid in Ballarat who obtained a job for him as a groom at a wage of just over £6 a month[151]. While it may have been far from the realisation of his dreams of the gold fields, it was at least more profitable.

There was one common thread among the emigrants who

The Mellon farmstead at Camphill forms part of the Ulster-American Folk Park. The family rose to considerable business prominence and helped establish the folk park at Omagh. *by kind permission of the Ulster American Folk Park, Omagh, Co Tyrone*

57

sought a future in business and commerce, however. Whether providing provisions or timber, sugar or railways, they all had the prospect – and the challenge – of opportunities to realise the emigrant's dream – that a better future awaited.

Often a hard-nosed business attitude was displayed by Ulster's emigrants, and this approach is sometimes seen as a characteristic of the often-dour Ulster settlers. Nowhere is there any better example of such an ethos – and the success which it brought – than in the story of the Mellon Brothers of Tyrone, whose legacy in Northern Ireland remains for visitors to view at the Ulster-American Folkpark at Camphill, Omagh. The Mellons were small farmers from west Tyrone, who emigrated to the United States in 1818, settling in Westmoreland County in Western Pennsylvania, already home to other family members. Land would hold the key to the success of Thomas Mellon, who was just five when his family left Tyrone, as he bought up real estate in addition to being a judge in Pittsburgh. When the city was devastated by fire in 1845, Thomas Mellon's land holdings assumed exceptional value. The Mellon dynasty had began and would continue, the Mellon National Bank of Pittsburgh being one underlining aspect of the great riches which they accrued. Thomas Mellon schooled his sons to follow in his footsteps and was a frugal man; he is reported to have advised his sons to make no friends and warned them against 'theatre-going, party going and writing letters to girls'.[152] If there is a typical example of a hard-nosed Ulsterman, canny with his money, it surely has to be Thomas Mellon (although the Mellons did, of course, establish foundations and trusts and helped establish the Ulster-American Folk Park).

The Mellons were not alone in the field of commercial success, although they were among the most prominent. One of the wealthiest businessmen in Australia, however, was Henry Osborne, who sold his farm in County Tyrone in 1829 and purchased linen from the profits, which he then shipped to Sydney. He had been one of a family of ten from the townland of Dirnaseer in Tyrone and followed two elder brothers to Australia. Within 30 years of his linen investment, Osborne had 315,000 acres of dairy land, a coalmine and a seat in the local parliament, and when he died he was described as the richest man in Australia.[153]

The name Getty is synonymous with wealth, and was another of those with Ulster connections that accrued wealth almost beyond comprehension. The first of the family in the United States was James, who was a native of Londonderry, and who bought land which would later be fought over by the armies of the Union and the Confederacy during the Civil War; Gettysburg remains a lasting legacy of his presence in the United States from 1780 onwards.[154] One author has remarked that 20th century oil king Paul Getty ". . . not only looked like an Ulster farmer, but behaved like one, keeping his women in order with promises about his will."[155] Whether others did the same or not, there would appear to be a common denominator between those who did exceptionally well in the field of wealth and those who got comfortably by; as canny Ulster-Scots, the emigrants and their descendents knew how to look after their money!

[102] Hans L Trefousse, *Andrew Johnson, A Biography*, 1991

[103] For an account of Timothy Eaton's life see Mary-Etta Macpherson, *Shopkeepers to a Nation*, Toronto, 1963

[104] *Larne Times* and *Weekly Telegraph*, 1929

[105] *Larne Times* and *Weekly Telegraph*, 4 March 1933

[106] I am grateful to David Verran, Local History Librarian, Auckland City Libraries, for the information supplied from the New Zealand Dictionary of Biography on the Entrican Brothers.

[107] *Larne Times* and *Weekly Telegraph*, 7 November 1903

[108] *Weekly Telegraph*, 5 December 1908

[109] *Weekly Telegraph*, 16 September 1905

[110] Research carried out by the Ballyclare Historical Society, 2001, see 'Ballynure's Link with a prominent American General', *Larne Times*, 3 January 2002

[111] *Larne Times*, 21 February 1931

[112] *Larne Times*, 9 June 1949

[113] *Larne Times*, 18 July 1963

[114] *Belfast Weekly Telegraph*, 8 December 1923

[115] *Larne Times*, 2 May 1946

[116] See *Broadisland Journal*, 2002, historical journal of Ballycarry Community Association

[117] Information from the late Mr Roy Sproule, Ballycarry, County Antrim, son-in-law of William Calwell

[118] *Larne Times*, 16 January 1926

[119] *Weekly Telegraph*, 21 June 1924

[120] *Weekly Telegraph*, 27 July 1929

[121] *Larne Times*, 1 April 1948, carries an account of the memoir of Joseph Hill

[122] see *Larne Times*, 'Sugar was foundation for Larne's most famous building', 27 February 2003

[123] Ancestor of the late Lord Hailsham, former Lord Chancellor

[124] *Larne Weekly Reporter*, 18 August 1877

[125] *Larne Times*, 22 December 1894

[126] *Belfast News Letter*, 24 April 1810

[127] *Larne Times*, 4 March 1993

[128] see Terry Coleman, *Passage to America*, Pimlico, London, 1972

[129] reported in the *Northern Whig* of Tuesday, 22 June 1847

[130] *Northern Whig*, 4 August 1948

[131] *Weekly Telegraph*, 6 January 1912

[132] *Weekly Telegraph*, 23 April 1904

[133] *Weekly Telegraph*, 31 March 1928

[134] *Weekly Telegraph*, 13 January 1912

[135] *Larne Times*, 4 September 1952

[136] *Weekly Telegraph*, 28 March 1925

[137] Coffey and Morgan, *Irish Families in Australia and New Zealand, 1788–1979*, Victoria, 1979

[138] *Larne Times*, 16 January 1926

[139] *Larne Times*, 18 May 1950

[140] Coffey and Morgan, ibid

[141] *Weekly Telegraph*, 6 July 1940

[142] *Northern Whig*, 18 December 1923

[143] *Larne Times*, 20 June 1946

[144] *Northern Whig*, 24 April 1847

[145] *Larne Times*, 20 July 1901

[146] *Northern Whig*, 19 October 1839

[147] *Northern Whig*, 16 January 1847

[148] *Weekly Telegraph*, 23 August 1945

[149] *Larne Times*, 26 February 1921

[150] *Belfast News Letter*, 26 August 1853

[151] Grenfell Morton, 'Ulster Emigrants to Australia', *Ulster Folklife*, Volume 18, 1972, p116

[152] Rory Fitzpatrick, *God's Frontiersmen. The Scots-Irish Epic*, London, 1989, p154–156

[153] 'Ulster people contributed to Australian success story', Lena Ferguson, *News Letter*, 11 January 1988

[154] Fitzpatrick, op cit, p154

[155] Fitzpatrick, p154

To be found in many fields: Exiles in diverse walks of life across the world

William Alexander Coulter was born in the Glens of Antrim in March 1849 and went to sea as a young teenager. He was apprenticed to a merchant ship's captain at the tender age of 13 years. Although William would not realise it initially, his time at sea was to prove highly beneficial in another crucial way.

For William Coulter is not remembered today as a seaman but an artist, and maritime art was his forte, prompted by long hours at sea when he had the time to observe and to sketch the scenes and ships around him. Arriving in San Francisco at the age of 20 in 1869, the young man from County Antrim decided to stay in the city and worked as a sail maker, also progressing his art. In 1874 his paintings first came to the attention of the wider public and were immediately highly regarded for their detail, Coulter thereafter becoming a regular exhibitor with the San Francisco Art Association.

In the late 1870s Coulter was to travel to Europe, where he studied with several well-known ship and marine painters. His paintings were highly regarded, not least by ship captains and ship owners, who appreciated particularly his accurate depictions of marine subjects.

In April 1882 a milestone in William Coulter's career as a painter was reached when he went to Hawaii, for what would be the first of several visits. That May his Californian and European seascapes were featured in an exhibition at the Honolulu Library and Reading Room. In September he held an auction sale of a selection of his work, including a few landscapes, with prices ranging from $20 to $100.

The effort was making his name known in Hawaii and his most important commission was to have a connection to the island; a series of five large maritime scenes, including a view of Honolulu harbour, was executed between 1909 and 1920 for the assembly room of the Merchants Exchange Building, now the Union Bank, in San Francisco. The five paintings were 16 feet by 18 feet mural panels and the Assembly Room where they were placed was centre of all trading and maritime business on the West Coast of the United States.

Coulter, who had family connections with Glenarm and Glenariff in County Antrim, remained the great maritime chronicler of the San Francisco Bay area for much of his life, one of his finest and most dramatic pieces detailing the Great Fire of 1906, which followed the earthquake.

He lived in the Sausalito district of San Francisco, his house being just a few feet from the water which he loved so much, and he also kept a studio at Montgomery Street in the city.

It was a feature of Coulter's work that he seldom painted a ship in distress, preferring to show them in harmony with their surroundings or in their full glory. From 1869 to 1936 he chronicled the shipping business of San Francisco, showing square-riggers, tug boats, schooners and many other vessels that sailed from and to the Golden Gate.

In 1896 Coulter had joined the staff of the *San Francisco Call* newspaper as their waterfront artist and his pen and ink drawings appeared daily in the newspaper until the disaster of 1906.

The renowned artist died at his California home on 13 March 1936. He had already been the subject of a commemorative stamp produced by the US Postal Service in 1923, featuring one of his paintings. In 1943 further commemoration was to occur when, appropriately enough, a ship built at the Kaiser Shipyard in San Francisco was named the SS *William A Coulter*. Even more appropriate was the fact that the vessel was built to help the war effort involving the US and her Allies, the most prominent of which was the United Kingdom, where young William Coulter had grown up on the shores of the Antrim Coast.[156]

William Coulter was one of those exiles who would be remembered in the arts field, but is perhaps not one of the better known of those of Ulster stock. When we examine the world of the arts for those of Ulster stock we often tend to think of those such as Edgar Allan Poe, one of the greatest (and darkest) writers of his generation, famed for works such as *The Raven*. It is believed that Poe's Ulster links come through his Ayrshire family and their movement into the north of Ireland, from whence would depart David Poe and his wife Sarah, who left County Cavan for America in 1742.[157]

Others followed the same writing profession of Poe, although they would not be as well remembered. William John Geddis, for example, was born in Belfast in 1860 and emigrated with his parents to Australia at the age of four years. At the age of 14 years he began a career in journalism, joining the *Auckland Star* and becoming a reporter at the age of 16 and later a sub-editor at the age of 28. Geddis later became editor of the *New Zealand Observer* for 20 years, while his brother James McRobert Geddis, who was born in 1856, had joined the staff of the *New Zealand Herald* in 1869, was editor of the *New Zealand Freelance* in 1900 and a Hansard writer between 1888 and 1921.[158] Joseph Medill, who died in San Antonio, Texas, in 1899, had been Editor-in-chief of the *Chicago Tribune* and was a native of Newbliss, County Monaghan. A successful public figure for many years, his will left nearly $5,000,000 to prove the point.[159] Arthur Anderson, who was proprietor of the *New York Sun* and a native of Carsonstown, Saintfield, endowed First Presbyterian Church in Londonderry with 1,000 volumes for its library and a course of lectures each winter for the benefit of the congregation, as well as leaving a substantial cheque for the Bible Class of the Second Presbyterian Church for establishment of a library and £200 to Greyabbey Presbyterian Church. Initially a teacher, he closed his books at Gwynnes Scholastic Institute in the Maiden City and emigrated to the United States in 1869, taking up the profession of journalism, and dying in his adopted city in 1913.[160]

Among those of influence in any society are teachers, and among those who left a classroom in Ulster for a new school across the ocean was Samuel McCready, who was principal teacher of a small country school at Blackhill, Magheramorne, County Antrim, for 14 years before emigrating with his wife to Saskatchewan in 1910. The departure was the subject of a presentation in the local Presbyterian Church, when a gold watch was handed over to the popular teacher.[161] McCready carried on the teaching profession in the small rural community of Bresaynor, Saskatchewan, and during the Second World War his younger son, Corporal Douglas McCready, then serving in the Royal Canadian Air Force, would retrace his father's steps back to Magheramorne.[162] Mary Jane Hutton had, like Samuel McCready, been a teacher prior to emigration, in her case to Philadelphia. In the 1860s she taught on the McGarel-Hogg estate at Magheramorne, and later married Hugh Hutton, who was stationmaster at Larne. The couple later moved to the USA, where she died at the advanced age of 84 years. Her six sons were pallbearers at the funeral at St Denis Roman Catholic Church, Philadelphia, in the summer of 1930.[163]

One teacher who returned home from exile was Hugh McCambridge, a Larne man, who trained as a teacher at the McKenna Memorial School in the town and emigrated to New Zealand. After spending 30 years there, however, he returned to his native town in 1949 to enjoy his retirement.[164] Similarly, John Watt Smyth, who had been a Judge of the Chief Court of the Punjab, returned in his retirement to his native Larne, where he was one of the more notable citizens.[165]

Another figure who was prominent in the legal profession was Glens of Antrim exile Richard Campbell. Born in 1870 and educated in a small schoolroom at Feystown near Glenarm, he emigrated to the United States as a boy of 14 and would enter Georgetown University, becoming involved in politics after his graduation. He was regarded as a brilliant writer, and an able lawyer, and when he was appointed to the Judge of the Supreme Court of America in the Philippines, one newspaper related that "He has risen to fame in a country where liberty is a watchword and there is a field for genius."[166] Among his friends who were political figures was Theodore Roosevelt, believed to have ancestral connections near Gleno, further south. Roosevelt appointed Campbell a Federal Attorney in the Philippines in 1906 and later a Judge there. Campbell had some noteworthy friends at home in Ireland, too, among them the poets William Butler Yeats and George Russell. In 1921 the Judge was secretary of the American Committee for Relief in Ireland and would later visit the Glens and be feted there at a Gaelic athletic event held in his honour. He died at the age of 56 in 1935, having apparently planned to return to visit County Antrim again.[167]

Others were less prominent in a national field, but significant in their own rights, among them George Walter Young, a native of Knockbawn, County Armagh, who was coroner of Christchurch, New Zealand, for many years prior to his death in 1869,[168] Belfastman William McCulloch, who was an accountant in Napier, New Zealand[169], Hugh Younge, an Attorney at Law in Chicago, who was a native of County Antrim and died in Ohio in 1953,[170] and Pat Maybin of Ballyclare, who was busily engaged in construction work for the American troops in Fiji during the Second World War.[171] Someone else who was deeply involved in construction work was TH Morrow, an Australian MP who was the managing director of the firm of TH Morrow & Co, which supplied building materials in the area around Sydney, and he was a prominent member of the Ulster Association in the city in the 1920s.[172] Many others reflected their remembrance of their homeland by trips back to their birthplace, a newspaper account from April 1929 detailing that Robert Gilliland of Larne was among them. He had arrived in Ulster via South Africa, where he had spent time visiting his brother, en route from Chile, where he was director and general manager of the Compania Sur Americana de Explosinos, one of the companies of the Nobel syndicate. Gilliland's story was something of a rags-to-riches affair, having started his business career in the shipping office at Larne Harbour and ending up as director of one of the major companies in South America at that time.[173]

Another Ulsterman who achieved considerable fame and prestige in his adopted land was Rhodesian High Court Judge Sir Robert McIlwaine, a native of Kilwaughter in County Antrim. He emigrated to South Africa in 1895 to enter the civil service in what was then Cape Colony, and it proved to be the start of a legal career which would see him reach the top level of the judiciary. In addition to his legal background, however, the Ulster exile was one of the first men to start

A plaque in Gleno village, County Antrim, commemorates the links the area has to US President Theodore (Teddy) Roosevelt. His Irvine and Craig ancestors were said to have come from the Gleno valley.

orange growing on a commercial scale in Rhodesia and a park northwest of Salisbury (now Harare in Zimbabwe) was named Lake McIlwaine in his honour.[174]

Another man from Larne also had a lake named after him. Thomas Woodside was from Pound Street in the town and emigrated to Sault Ste Marie in Ontario in 1923, where he gained employment as an aircraft engineer. Two years later he joined the temporary staff of the provincial air service and in 1928 received his pilot's licence. A member of the aerial photographic department, his task was to locate forest fires in Ontario's extensive wooded areas, and attempt to have them put out before they took serious hold. One of the tasks which he also performed was the mapping out of the Lake Superior route of the Trans-Canadian Highway, which was completed 30 years later. Promotion followed and he retired as Forest Fire Protection Engineer in 1961 after 36 years service. Thomas Woodside was a popular local resident, topping the poll in his electoral district when he stood for election to the Memorial Gardens Commission and winning the seat easily.[175] The naming of a lake in Quetico Provincial Park in Ontario is one of the more unique ways Ulster exiles in Canada are recalled.

Many emigrants in Canada and elsewhere gravitated towards those with similar roots, and this would appear to have been the case in New York, where JO Henderson was a senior official in linen circles. A native of Larne, he was friendly with another Larne man, Whitford Kane, one of the prominent actors of his day, and often saw him, according to a contemporary newspaper account.[176] Few would meet up, however, in such unique circumstances than did Nat McWilliam and Dave Hunter in 1946. McWilliam was the engineer on the Newport ferry in Victoria, Australia, while Hunter was skipper of a vessel called the *Southern Collins*, which sailed into the port. Captain Hunter asked the first man he met on the pier if he knew his old friend from County Antrim and was pointed in the direction of McWilliam, who also happened to be on the pier at the same time. The men had last been in each other's company 30 years before, and both had been educated in a little country school at Crosshill near Larne.[177]

Another connection with shipping comes in the form of a Scottish man who had connections with the Belfast shipyards. HS Henderson's death in Matabeleland was reported in newspapers in Northern Ireland in 1942, when it was detailed

Andrew Barry Moore, descendant of County Antrim emigrants to Pennsylvania, was the first medical doctor in Spartanburg County, South Carolina. This replica of his surgery stands at Walnut Grove plantation in the state.

Sporting achievements also brought recognition for some emigrants, such as Portglenone exile JH Wright, who found a new life and sporting fame in New York, easily winning races at the Brooklyn Athletic Club awards in 1900.[180] James McCashin, a native of Randalstown, County Antrim, was also a well-known figure in the sporting circuit, being a soccer enthusiast but also a breeder and importer of racehorses. He was also reputed to have been the first importer of Kerry Blue terriers into the United States.[181]

John Reid of Carrickfergus provides an example of how hard-working Ulster emigrants bettered their lot. His involvement with horses was not a sporting one as was James McCashin's, for he was a blacksmith in the town of New Westminster in British Columbia in 1877 and later established his own company, the Westminster Iron Works Co, which would later be controlled by two of his sons, William and John. The elder John Reid had gone into partnership in 1886 to form a small iron works and had built the first four-wheeled stagecoaches used in British Columbia, and, later, steam engines for ferries on the route to Vancouver. A newspaper article in his native district in 1948 noted that the farmer's son from Carrickfergus had built up a firm, which had played a major part in the industrial development of the Far West of Canada.[182] In 1906, meanwhile, a Belfast boy named Thomas Cunningham was at the start of his working life in New York. Employed as an elevator boy in a large hotel in the city, his courage during a major fire, resulted in lives being saved and he was hailed as a boy hero after he continued to run his elevator to save people when stairwells had been closed by the flames. The 17 year-old suffered burns to his hands and face, but the *New York Herald* reported that:

> For nearly half an hour Cunningham stuck to his post, until the fire sweeping up the shaft had heated the elevator to the smoking point and parts of the structure were burning. The lower three floors of the building were wrecked and the three upper floors were saved by the firemen only after two hours of hard fighting.[183]

Not all Ulster's emigrants would be heroes like Thomas Cunningham. But most of them would share in common that they would face a hard struggle to do well in the various lands of their adoption. Larne man John Hill, happily settled in Canada in 1958, would reflect that:

> Canada's aura as a land of plenty has caused many a heartache before and will continue to do so until people arriving here divorce themselves from the idea that all they have to do is buy a steamship ticket to easy living[184]

Easy living may have been a dream, but for most emigrants, whatever walk of life and wherever they choose to settle, the chance of a better lifestyle was well worth working towards.

that he had donated the profits of several of his gold mines in Rhodesia to the war effort when the conflict broke out. He had also presented a seaside home in Cape Province as a holiday resort for RAF men training in Rhodesia at the time. It was noted that the mine owner had left Belfast in 1892 and that during the South African conflict he was awarded the Victoria Cross for bravery in action with the Rhodesia Horse.[178] The vast bulk of Ulster emigrants would not, of course, own nor have shares in gold mines, but some would find fame in other ways. In 1908, for example, the *Moose Jaw Evening Times* in Canada would report that engineer John McAllister, a native of Gleno in County Antrim, was among those on a steam train which had delivered a record time for a 110 mile journey. McAllister and the Conductor, a man named Milliken, had completed the journey between the railway station at Swift Current and Moose Jaw in 112 minutes, beating previous records by over nine minutes.[179]

In the early years of settlement on the American frontier the role of professions such as apothecary was a highly significant one, administering medical help to those who had to survive not only harsh conditions and hard work but also snakes and other hazards. Here re-enactor Eric Williams of Greenwood, South Carolina, exhibits the type of medicines which an 18th century apothecary would have carried.

156 Information supplied by James Murray, late of Glenarm, an emigrant himself to Sweden, and from San Francisco archives

157 see 'Edgar Allan Poe's Ulster-Scots connection' by Robert Densmore Brill, in *The Ulster Scot*, November 2003

158 Coffey and Morgan, *Irish Families in Australia and New Zealand 1788–1979*, Victoria, 1979

159 *Weekly Telegraph*, 15 April 1899

160 *Weekly Telegraph*, 6 September 1913

161 *Larne Times*, 23 April 1910

162 *Larne Times*, 26 April 1945

163 *Larne Times*, 28 June 1930

164 *Larne Times*, 23 June 1949

165 *Larne Times*, 18 May 1949

166 Felix McKillop, *Glenarm. A Local History*, Belfast 1987, p74

167 *New York Times*, 17 October 1935; McKillop, op cit, p74

168 *Belfast News Letter*, 16 November 1869

169 *Weekly Telegraph*, 28 March 1903

170 *Larne Times*, 19 February 1953

171 *Larne Times*, 27 December 1945

172 *Weekly Telegraph*, 30 January 1926

173 *Larne Times*, 6 April 1929

174 see, for example, 'More Memories of Sir Robert McIlwaine', *Larne Times*, June 15, 1989

175 *Daily Star*, Sault Ste Marie, 3 December 1957

176 *Larne Times*, 29 July 1948

177 *Larne Times*, 4 July 1946

178 *Belfast Weekly Telegraph*, 13 August 1942

179 *Weekly Telegraph*, 14 March 1908

180 *Weekly Telegraph*, 6 October 1900

181 *Weekly Telegraph*, 14 April 1934

182 *Larne Times*, 1 April 1948

183 *Weekly Telegraph*, 3 March 1906

184 *Larne Times*, 21 August 1958

Spreading the word:
Clerics and congregations abroad

The manse of a South African Presbyterian cleric provided a strong clue as to his origins in the 1920s. For when it was built for him in 1921 Rev Dr JJ McClure named it 'Dalriada' in honour of the ancient kingdom which had once existed in North Antrim around the 6th century and included part of Scotland in its realms. The new 'Dalriada', located at Cape Town, South Africa, was a reminder that Ulster exiles did not forget their homeland, and the fact of its being a church manse no doubt helped to emphasise to the wider congregational and city community of the links which their pastor had with the British Isles.

McClure was one of many Ulstermen who rose to distinction in clerical positions across the world. He was born in 1860 and died in 1925, and was the son of Rev Samuel McClure of Crossroads, County Londonderry, while his mother's Smyth family was prominent in Dervock, North Antrim. JJ McClure went to Magee College and New College, Edinburgh, was licensed for the Presbyterian ministry in 1883 and ordained that same year at Duneane in County Antrim. The following year he married Miss Denham, daughter of the previous minister of the church, and over a decade later, in 1896, he accepted a call which came from Gardens Presbyterian Church in Cape Town. The congregation grew with the colony, and in 1901 a new church building was opened to accommodate 472 people, the foundation stone being laid by Lord Milner of Capetown and St James, the King's High Commissioner in South Africa.[185]

Dr McClure became an influential figure in the land of his adoption, both in church and public life, and, in 1906, he was elected Moderator of the Presbyterian General Assembly in South Africa, and awarded the degree of Doctor of Divinity at home by the Presbyterian Theological College in Belfast. The exile made regular visits to the General Assembly of the church in Ireland, and used such occasions to visit family and friends including Mrs Smyth of Dhu Varren, Portstewart. His brother had also followed an emigrant's path, meanwhile, and was a banker in New York City, while McClure's two sons, Jack and Cecil, served in the Great War, paying the price for their loyalty to the Empire; Jack died in London of wounds received, while Cecil was killed in action.[186]

McClure was just one of those exiles who were prominent in church circles in various parts of the world. Rev TH Spratt, who was appointed Bishop of Wellington, New Zealand, in 1911, for example, was a native of Dromore, County Down, and had a distinguished career at Trinity College, Dublin, before going to St Barnabas Church, Auckland, in 1886, and subsequently taking up the charge of St Pauls, Wellington, in 1892.[187] Another distinguished Ulster cleric under the Southern Cross was Rev William Marcus Dill Mackey, who was Moderator of the General Assembly of New South Wales in 1889 and prominent in the Australian Protestant Defence Association.[188] He was born in Lisfannon, County Donegal, in June 1849 and educated at Londonderry, including Magee College. His first church was at Draperstown and during his distinguished career in Australia it was said that he "worked heart and soul to rouse the Protestant spirit".[189] As was the case with McClure, Mackey had a family background in the church, and the family had supplied ministers for the Presbyterian Church over two generations. Rev Robert Erwin, who was a Belfast man, was an emigrant to New Zealand in 1883 and became Moderator of the Presbyterian Church in New Zealand in 1897.[190]

Rev Rutherford Waddell, who was born at Glenarm on the Antrim Coast in 1849, was nephew of the famous Ulster author Captain Mayne Reid and later made a mark for himself in New Zealand. He had emigrated in 1877, having studied at Queen's University and theology college in Belfast. Two years later he was ordained at St Andrew's Church in Dunedin, remaining there for 40 years and gaining a reputation as a social reformer on account of his campaigns against the appalling working conditions which the working classes in the city faced. Waddell's exertions resulted in a Royal Commission being set up and laws being brought in to alleviate conditions for ordinary families. The Glens man was also founder and first editor of the *Outlook* newspaper, official weekly newspaper of the Presbyterian Church in New Zealand, and he also formed the New Zealand Prison Reform Association and involved himself in other social campaigns of the day. He died in April 1932, some years after having the honour of being awarded an honorary doctorate by the Belfast Theological College. A son of the manse himself,

Waddell extended his Christian doctrine into the area of social reform in a way which would have lasting benefit for those least able to campaign for themselves.[191]

Thomas Holden, who achieved prominence within the Presbytery of Los Angeles in the United States and also the Synod of California, was born at Ballyrickard near Larne in 1896 and emigrated to Pasadena, California, in 1914. As a young man he decided to enter the Presbyterian ministry and had a 43-year career, starting at Highland Park Presbyterian Church in Los Angeles in 1924. Five years later he was at Wilshire Crest Presbyterian Church and was elected assistant clerk to the Synod of California, eventually becoming the Clerk to the Synod in 1932 and holding the post until 1967, also holding other significant positions over the same period, among them President of the Board of San Francisco Theological Seminary between 1951 and 1965 (it was said that the green hillsides of the campus reminded him of his native land).

Holden was a much respected ecumenical leader and undertook pioneering dialogue with Roman Catholics a quarter of a century before the Second Vatican Council; it was said that he inherited this liberal approach from his father John, who had been an elder in Clogher Presbyterian Church in County Tyrone. His son would later be a leading light in the Synod of California, which dissolved as a unit with nearly 600 churches in December 1967 at the time of Holden's own retirement. The Ulster exile, who died in 1992, is a good example of a figure significant within a wider church community, although not necessarily prominent at national level.[192]

Similarly, many churches have owed much to Ulster emigrants for their foundations in far-flung parts of the world. The United States is a good example because of the mass emigration of Presbyterians from the north of Ireland in the 18th and, to a much lesser extent, the 19th centuries. Nazareth Presbyterian in South Carolina, which is sited near the city of Spartanburg, is a good example of the role County Antrim settlers played in the New World. Families such as the Andersons, Snoddys, Moores, Barrys, Caldwells and others helped found two settlements in a 20-mile radius – Moore and Wellford. When a church was to be built it was decided to establish its location by having members of the fledgling congregation walk from both settlements; where they met, the Nazareth Church was built, a spring close at hand being part of the criteria since it was needed to refresh horses and congregation on the Sabbath after their trek to church. The land on which the church was built was granted

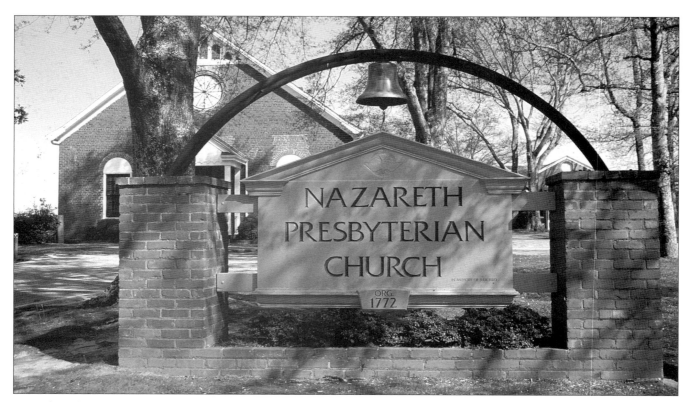

Nazareth Presbyterian Church, South Carolina, one of many founded by Ulster settlers in the Upcountry district of the state.

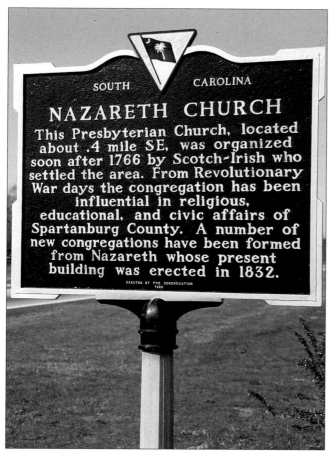

An historical marker near Nazareth Presbyterian Church highlights the role the congregation has played in the life of the area.

The cemetery of Nazareth Presbyterian Church near Spartanburg, South Carolina, has familiar surnames on the stones; Patrick Crawford died during the American Revolution and was killed during a skirmish with Loyalists, when his best friend mistook him for one of the enemy.

to the congregation by one John Caldwell, and in the 1990s the original log cabin which he had built was 'discovered' intact inside a later building, and painstakingly taken down and reassembled in the church grounds to be used for the local Scout group. Nazareth Church, as a historical marker nearby states, was organised soon after 1766 by Ulster-Scots settlers and has played a prominent part in the religious, educational and civic affairs of Spartanburg County since the Revolutionary War.[193]

There are many other examples in the United States of the role played by emigrants in church foundation. James and Jannet Gillespy and their family had moved to County Antrim from Kirkcudbright in Scotland before emigrating to Augusta County in Virginia. There they helped form the Tinkling Spring Presbyterian Church.[194] The Lyles of Raloo, County Antrim, also ended up in Virginia, and were to play a formative role in the early life of Timber Ridge Presbyterian Church, and the list goes on.[195] Hugh Millar Thompson, who became a Bishop in the Protestant Episcopal Church

in Mississippi, was born at Tamlaght near Londonderry in 1830 and emigrated with his parents John T Thompson and Anne Miller, settling in Ohio. The Londonderry man held many clerical appointments during a distinguished career and was also editor of a number of church publications as well as being author of several religious books. Like quite a number of fellow exiles, he paid tribute to those of Ulster stock, describing them as "steadfast, stalwart, true to conviction, tough brained but tender hearted".[196]

Undoubtedly the most prominent clerical figure who made his name outside his native land was Dr Alexander Irvine, whose books *My Lady of the Chimney Corner* and *The Souls of Poor Folk* are classics in their own right and tell the story of triumph of the spirit over poverty in his native Antrim

67

Bullock Creek Presbyterian Church was one of the early congregations established by Ulster settlers in the Upcountry region of South Carolina.

town and most particularly the story of his mother and family at Pogue's Entry there. He was one of 12 children born at Pogue's Entry, five of whom died in infancy. His father was a cobbler and the family often experienced hunger in their lives. Irvine took a job as a newspaper boy at the age of eight to earn money for the rest of the family. He would later obtain employment along with three of his brothers in a coal mine in Scotland, and then joined the Royal Marines.[197] Irvine would gradually better his education by reading classical novels and listening to the speech of the officers in the Royal Navy with whom he came into contact. He would later leave the Marines and return to Antrim for a time before emigrating to New York, where a missionary calling directed him to the Bowery, a notorious district of the city.[198] In the Bowery he fought relentlessly for the relief of poverty and for social relief and soon won support across the United States. His view of the rough people of the Bowery with whom he came into contact was probably coloured by his statement that "We are all rough hewn people, and the fine edges were few and hard to find."[199]. Soon Irvine became known to many as 'the Fighting Parson' because of his stand against poverty, and this would become doubly relevant when the First World War broke out and he was appointed Chief Morale Officer

of the Allied Armies, 1916–18. When he died in Hollywood, USA, in 1941 it was noted by one Ulster newspaper that "His whole life was tribute to Ulster grit and perseverance"[200] A later author from his native town noted that:

> All his life, Alexander Irvine fought and suffered for the well-being of the poorest of the poor upon whose back are always borne the world's heaviest burdens.[201]

Irvine himself would return to his native land one last time. But the return of his ashes was postponed by the war and it was not until 1946 that a funeral service in his native town would see hundreds flock to pay their tribute to an author whose work *My Lady of the Chimney Corner* was in itself a lasting tribute to his mother. Underneath a stone bearing the words of her philosophy 'Love is Enough', the ashes of one of the most distinguished Ulstermen of his era were interred, appropriately enough bringing his life in a full circle back to Pogue's Entry. It was recounted in a contemporary weekly newspaper that:

> There were few to bid farewell when young Alexander Irvine left Antrim many years ago, but there were hundreds in the main street to await his homecoming, and salute the memory of a great soul[202]

There were doubtless many hundreds of Ulster exiles who played a part in the ministry of their respective churches in various parts of the world, and most of them did not attract prominence on the scale of Alexander Irvine but carried out their calling faithfully and diligently in their own parishes and congregations. The Rev Dr William Freeland, for example, a native of Clontibret, County Monaghan, would be well known in Alymer, Canada, for his preaching,[203] while another Canadian cleric of distinction in his local area was Rev JC Ross, son of a Ballymena farmer, who was minister of Knox Presbyterian Church, Waterdown, Ontario, and in 1935 filled the position as Moderator of the Presbytery of Hamilton.[204] Hugh Clyde McCready, who died in Hamilton, New Zealand in 1933 at the age of 80, was one of the founders of the Auckland Unitarian Church, the first of its kind in New Zealand.[205] Rev Dr AK McMinn of Victoria, British Columbia, was among those who played a significant part in the negotiations which brought about the merger of the Presbyterian, Methodist and Congregational churches into the United Church of Canada in 1925, and was a native of Straid near Ballyclare, County Antrim.[206]

In the United States, among them was Rev PM McKenna, who was pastor to the congregation of St Monica's Church in Barre, Vermont, and a County Antrim man,[207] Rev Robert Stevenson, a native of Rathconville, Poyntzpass, County Armagh, who ministered in Pittsburgh in the 1870s,[208] and Portadown native Rev J Newnham Mackenzie, who was appointed Archdeacon of Oklahoma in 1933. In his homeland he had been associated with the Waringstown area and also All Saints Parish Church in Belfast, where he was a Diocesan Lay Reader. His move across the Atlantic first took him to Canada in 1906, and this was followed by the decision to cross the border into the United States in 1911.[209]

Among many other Ulstermen who were prominent in their own adopted communities was Rev John Elder, a Belfastman who entered Omaha University and Omaha Presbyterian Seminary in the 1920s. He entered the Presbyterian ministry in Council Bluffs Presbytery, Iowa, in 1926.[210] Rev Joseph Boyd, who came from a prominent Larne Methodist family, became minister of a Methodist Episcopal Church at Texarkana in Texas,[211] while another relative, Dr James Boyd Brady, was a major figure in Methodism in Boston and was pastor of the People's Temple, then the largest Methodist Church in the world. He was also a missionary and visited China. An article in *The Christian Advocate* of 7 April 1894, details that Brady had been apprenticed to a trade before deciding to embark on a teaching career, working in schools in Portaferry and Ballymena before emigrating to the United States. Entering the ministry of the Methodist Episcopal Church, he moved from Newark, New Jersey, to Boston in 1893 and headed a revival of Methodism in the city, bringing between 7,000 and 10,000 worshippers per week to his services at the People's Temple.[212]

When James Augustine McFaul was a baby his parents took him on a journey far from the small townland at Rory's Glen, Kilwaughter, County Antrim, where he had been born. Family tradition has it that as they crossed Shane's Hill towards Ballymena in the 1850s, his father held his baby above his head for a last look at Kilwaughter in the distance. The family was Roman Catholic and their journey would eventually take them to Trenton, New Jersey, where James Augustine McFaul would rise to become the Bishop of Trenton and a prominent figure within the Roman Catholic Church in the United States. Like James Boyd, he did not forget the congregation which had nurtured his parents faith at home in Ireland; Boyd and McFaul both provided beautiful stained glass windows in Larne's Methodist and St MacNissi's Churches respectively.[213]

In 1906 McFaul was on the way to a meeting of senior clerics in Rome and took the opportunity to visit his home district once more, where he was lauded as "one of the most distinguished of their exiled children". The purpose was the dedication of the large memorial windows depicting the crucifixion which he had erected there in memory of his parents, but while he participated in a Mass at the church at Agnew Street in the town, McFaul was able to also visit relatives at Rory's Glen, left so many years before.[214]

Another highly prominent Ulster exile was the Roman Catholic Bishop of New York, John Joseph Hughes, who was born in 1797 near Augher in County Tyrone. His family left Ulster for Pennsylvania, at least partly because of the religious disqualifications which they found themselves under at the time as Catholics, and the story is told of how when his aunt Mary died, the local priest could not enter the cemetery to conduct her funeral because all denominations had to be buried within the regulations of the Established Church.[215] Such a situation would remain alive in the folk memory of those who suffered it as a community, as indeed did the Presbyterians, long after the Penal Laws had died away.

One of the more long-lived of the emigrant clerics was Dr Andrew Malcolm Morrison, born in Belfast in 1820, was minister of a church at home for some 40 years. He subsequently emigrated to California, then went to Kansas, where he practised medicine for a time before becoming a professor at a university. When he reached 100 Morrison had married for the fourth time, his bride being 72 year-old Mary Augusta Barney. He died in 1924 at the tremendous age of 103 years, having put down his long life to laughter, even temper and only the necessary amount of sleep.[216]

Historical records show that many emigrants did not forget those at home when providing their wills, and among those who reflected this in terms of his religious background was Thomas Martin, who died in Jamaica in 1839. He had been a grocer and spirit dealer at home in Belfast, and in his Last Will and Testament left twenty pounds – a reasonable sum in those days – for the benefit of the Roman Catholic

Church in Donegall Street, Belfast, "to which he belonged and in the faith of which he departed from this world".[217] The importance of faith to those abroad is highlighted in the letters of John McKenty of Glenarm, a ship's doctor, who although not an emigrant, provides something of the experience of all those travelling overseas. McKenty, also writing in 1839, notes in his letters to his mother from Bonny River in Nigeria that:

> We have no clergyman nor any house of worship within 1000 miles. I beg that you will remember me in your prayers when at Mass, as I will not have the opportunity of hearing Mass till my arrival in England.[218]

Sadly the ship's doctor died in Nigeria in 1841 on his second voyage to Africa. Although his experience of the lack of a place to worship was not as pronounced in the American colonies, many settlers found themselves on the frontiers where circuit preachers would visit, sometimes infrequently. It is not surprising that, their religious faith being of considerable significance to the settlers, churches should be among the first structures erected and that these, in turn, would be utilised as schoolrooms. As Brown and Sorrells point out in their recent work, in the context of Presbyterian emigrants this emphasis on education created 'pathways to power' in Virginia – a process which perhaps helps explain an early predominance of Scotch-Irish figures in wider American political, religious and social life.[219]

The connection between Presbyterian dissent and the American Revolution is clearly highlighted if you visit the Waxhaw cemetery in South Carolina. There you will see the gravestone of Thomas McDow, who, as well as being Ruling Elder of the Waxhaw Church, was also a private in the South Carolina militia during the Revolutionary War. His example is just one of many. The church also appears to have inculcated leadership values in other fields; David Archibald, who was born in Londonderry, settled in Truro, Nova Scotia, in 1762, where in addition to being elder in the local Presbyterian Church, he was also the area's first Member of Parliament four years later. Another member of the family, AG Archibald, was also the first Governor of Manitoba.[220]

In Pittsburgh, one of the Ulster-Scot capitals of the Americas, the Ulster Society of Pittsburgh was founded in September 1913, apparently to promote the unionist cause against Home Rule in Ireland. On the anniversary of the signing of the Ulster Covenant each year the Society held a dinner, and among those involved were several prominent Belfast and area figures, including two clergymen, Rev EM McFadden DD, a native of Larne, and Rev Dr Evans, who was chaplain, and a Old Boy of the Belfast Royal Academical Institution.[221] Ten other clergymen were involved in the Society which, it was said, was "a power in the Pittsburgh community".

Somewhat less prominent, but no less mindful of his roots, was County Antrim man James Wilson, who settled

in Australia. After some 35 years he returned to his native district and received an address from the Minister, Session and Committee of Magheramorne Presbyterian Church, County Antrim. Wilson had also made a generous gesture to the church, however, purchasing a clock from a Royal Avenue firm in Belfast to present to his old congregation.[222]

There were, of course, many like Wilson who were not clerics and whose involvement in congregations and churches is somewhat concealed by history. Dr WG Price, organist and choirmaster of St George's Parish Church, Belfast, in the early 1900s, emigrated to Melbourne and became the city organist there the following year.[223] In many instances it is only through their prominence in other areas of life that we learn of the obviously strong church connections which operated for them. In other instances we know little if anything about the role they played. In 1853, for example, a memorial came back to Belfast from a number of Presbyterian settlers in Tamaki district, near Auckland in New Zealand, asking for a clergyman to be sent to minister to them. We

The gravestone of Thomas McDow at Waxhaw epitomises the clear links between Presbyterian churches and the Revolutionary cause in the United States.

know little about those who signed the memorial, more about the outcome: Rev John Macky, minister of Fahan in County Donegal, was appointed to make the journey to Auckland and establish a congregation the following spring.[224] Similarly, in 1839 the Secessionist Congregation of Larne held a soiree in their meeting house to bid farewell to one of their number, William S McCaughey, who was about to depart for Australia. While he may have been a faithful member of the Larne congregation and undoubtedly joined another congregation in his new home, history tells us little about William McCaughey thereafter.[225]

While emigrants might differ in their religious outlooks and their beliefs, it is clear that they held one thing above all in common; they had a sincere faith which was sustaining on journeys that crossed oceans and saw much hardship in new lands. In a strange land and a new world the call to worship and the religious ritual associated with the old land was of crucial importance. In the midst of sea journeys and unknown landscapes the 'rock of ages' still dwelt secure in their hearts. Perhaps the hymn *What a friend we have in Jesus* is doubly significant in that context. For, aside from its religious message, it was written by Joseph Scriven, who was born near Banbridge, County Down, in 1820 and became an emigrant to Canada. In 2002 a memorial window in his honour was unveiled at the church he attended, Seapatrick Parish Church, Banbridge, by his great-great-nephew, Bishop Henry Scriven.[226]

At Holy Trinity Church in Preston, Australia, a memorial tablet to an Ulster exile was erected in 1919. WE Holden, a builder, had been responsible for the erection of many public buildings in the town and in the city of Melbourne, it was reported, as well as being a faithful member of the church community and one of its great benefactors. The same newspaper which carried the account of his memorial tablet also detailed a memorial service at Port Chambers in New Zealand to Robert J Pullin, a Salvation Army official and a native of Larne.[227] Whether they have lasting memorials or not, however, Ulster exiles have undoubtedly played important parts in the life of their various churches and denominations abroad.

A memorial window in Indiantown Presbyterian Church, South Carolina, to Janet Witherspoon Wilson, descendant of Ulster families who settled the area in the 1730s.

185 *Weekly Telegraph*, 28 September 1901
186 *Weekly Telegraph*, 30 May 1925
187 *Weekly Telegraph*, 1 April 1911
188 *Weekly Telegraph*, 29 November 1913
189 ibid., 29 November 1913
190 Coffrey and Morgan, *Irish Families in Australia and New Zealand 1788–1879*, Victoria , 1979
191 *Larne Times*, 1 April 1971
192 Papers of Marshall Holden, Portland, Oregon, son of the late Rev Dr Thomas Holden, February 1999
193 See for example 'Raloo man's cabin is on the move in Spartanburg County', *Larne Times*, March 17, 1994
194 Billy Kennedy, *Scots Irish in the Shenandoah Valley*, Belfast, 1996, p136
195 Kennedy, p160
196 *The Ulster Scot*, March 2003
197 *East Antrim Times*, 23 March 1973
198 ibid., 30 March 1973
199 Alexander Irvine, *The Souls of Poor Folk*, Appletree Press, 1981, p102
200 *Larne Times*, 3 May 1941
201 Alastair Smyth in the foreword to *The Souls of Poor Folk*, 1981, p10
202 *Larne Times*, 1 August 1946
203 *Belfast News Letter*, 13 February 1873
204 *Weekly Telegraph*, 11 January 1936
205 *Larne Times*, 17 March 1994
206 *Larne Times*, 10 November 1949
207 *Weekly Telegraph*, 3 April 1926
208 A death notice for Stevenson appears in the *Belfast News Letter*, 10 March 1874
209 *Weekly Telegraph*, 10 June 1933
210 *Weekly Telegraph*, 4 September 1926
211 *Larne Times*, 23 October 1909
212 *Larne Times*, 10 October 1991
213 Both churches have heritage plaques outside to mark the connection with the American clerics
214 *Larne Times* and *Weekly Telegraph*, 1 September 1906
215 Grace F Fraser, 'Keeping the Faith: The Catholic Church and Education in Northern Ireland and the USA', Fitzpatrick and Ickringill, Atlantic Crossroads, Colourpoint, Newtownards, 2001, p87
216 *Weekly Telegraph*, 1 March 1924
217 *Belfast News Letter*, 10 September 1839
218 John McKenty correspondence, August 1839, Public Record Office, Belfast, T3627/2/3
219 Katharine L Brown and Nancy T Sorrells, 'Presbyterian Pathways to Power: Networking, Gentrification and the Scotch-Irish Heritage among Virginia Presbyterian Ministers, 1760–1860', in Fitzgerald and Ickringill, Atlantic Crossroads, Colourpoint, Newtownards, 2001
220 Rev Stuart Acheson, 'The Scotch Irish in Canada', Scotch-Irish Congress proceedings, Louisville, Kentucky, 1891, published Tennessee 1891, pps 195–212
221 *Weekly Telegraph*, 20 January 1917
222 *Larne Times*, 12 January 1895
223 *Weekly Telegraph*, 7 February 1925
224 *Belfast News Letter*, 30 December 1853
225 *Northern Whig*, 19 October 1839
226 *Belfast Telegraph*, 27 April 2002
227 *Weekly Telegraph*, 10 May 1919

Fraternal greetings: Travelling warrants and universal handshakes

The Reuter News Agency reported from Toronto in July 1925 that around 10,000 Orangemen had paraded through the city to mark the anniversary of the Battle of the Boyne. The report noted:

> The usual procession was diverted from its customary route in consideration of the illness of Mr Peter Ryan, a prominent Catholic, who in former years had always displayed the Orange colours outside his residence on the Twelfth.[228]

The story highlights that one of the prominent elements of Protestant life in Ulster – the Orange Order and celebrations of William of Orange – remained an important part of emigrant life in Protestant districts and settlements abroad in the 19th and 20th centuries. It also relates that in the case of Peter Ryan, there was no antagonism associated with these 'Old Country' celebrations; this was something which would not always be the case, for clashes would occur between Orangemen and Hibernians in New York, Canada, and elsewhere in the 19th century. It should be no surprise, however, that there was a link between the Orange and the Green outside Ireland: both fraternities helped provide a grounding and a base for emigrants seeking a new life and occupations in strange lands.

Because of the numbers involved, the largest identifiable fraternity in the context of Ulster emigrants was undoubtedly the Orange Order, and some idea of its influence can be gauged from the fact that prior to 1920 one in three of Canadian Protestant males was a member of the Order[229]. Whenever a member of a lodge in the North of Ireland was emigrating he was given a 'Travelling Certificate' which certified that he was in good standing with his home lodge and this was then used to transfer to a lodge in Canada, Australia, or wherever else he might be settling. One such travelling certificate, for Alexander Clarke, who belonged to Magheramorne Orange Lodge in County Antrim, has survived in the Canadian archives and highlights how the fraternal networks operated across the world. Clarke was welcomed with open arms into his new lodge in Ontario and would become a prominent member. He had joined the Orange Order in 1847 and died in 1885, his funeral service being conducted by his Orange Lodge, LOL 47, members from other lodges acting as pall bearers.[230] Alexander Clarke had a brother, who was more famous in Ontario Orange circles, since James Clarke rose to the position of Grand Master of the Provincial Grand Lodge of Ontario East. He was born at Magheramorne, and joined the Orange Order in Canada in 1848. A teacher by profession, Clarke emigrated to Canada in 1847, the same year as his brother, and settled at Bytown (later Ottawa), where he became one of Ottawa's most honoured and respected citizens, according to an article in the *Dominion Illustrated* in 1890 when he was

An old Orange sash from Canada LOL 1684 in Toronto. Symbols common to Orangeism elsewhere are displayed alongside those of the Canadian flag and a beaver. The sash was manufactured by the Whitehead & Hoag company of Newark, New Jersey.

James Clarke, a native of Magheramorne, County Antrim, who became the Provincial Grand Master of Ontario East in Canada.

Tom Stewart and George Stewart, descendants of Ulster settlers in Ontario, were members of Algonquin LOL, which was based in a mining community and, somewhat uniquely, met underground. Photo supplied by Gordon Sample, Ontario.

elected Grand Master. The paper said that the Grand Master was known as a Protestant of the staunchest Presbyterian type, and in politics a pronounced Conservative. "In the City of Ottawa and County of Carleton for many years past the name of Mr James Clarke has been a familiar one in every Orange and Protestant household" a contemporary Canadian newspaper stated. [231]

There were many thousands of Orangemen from the North of Ireland who ended up in Canada, helping to boost the numbers in lodges there, and just as many emigrants from the south, who also found a spiritual home in a lodge; it is a group of Protestant emigrants from Tipperary, for example, who are credited with formation of the first Orange lodge in Montreal. [232] Because of the sheer numbers involved, details are often sparse on individuals, although much work has been done on Orangeism, generally, in Canada,[233] and some of it identifies individuals, such as a highly interesting social and historical study by Gary Dennis, who focuses on the area of Muskota, Ontario.[234] In relation to one of the most prominent Orangemen of the district, the author tells us that:

None ever came close, however, to the fervency and devotion of James Clark of Monsell PO in Macauley township. Born, appropriately enough, on July 12 1839 in County Tyrone, Ireland, he joined the Orange Society on his 17th birthday and never missed a celebration of the Battle of the Boyne until 1932. He failed to make the walk that year because he died on June 7th. His obituary claimed that his record of attendance at Twelfth celebrations was probably unequalled in Ontario.[235]

There are many individual accounts in local newspapers of Ulster settlers and their links with the largest Protestant fraternity in the world. Among them is an account from 1906 of the departure of a member of Larne Total Abstinence LOL 766 for the land of the Maple Leaf, a travelling bag being presented as a compliment to the man, whose surname was McConnell.[236] A departure of an altogether different nature was reported in a weekly newspaper in 1918:

The death of Mr Charles McKendry took place on Sunday, September 9th, in the hospital at Edmonton, Alberta. The body arrived at Lashburn on Tuesday morning and

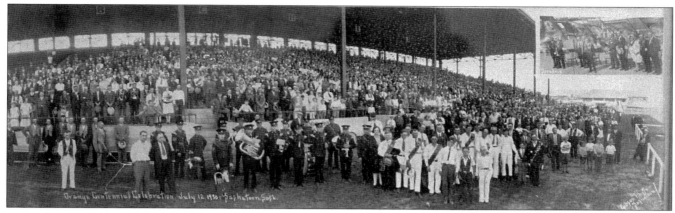

Gathered at Saskatoon, Saskatchewan, for the 1930 Twelfth. The Orange Order in Canada was a natural focus for Protestant Irish emigrants, although it did attract those of other backgrounds.

was received by the officers and members of Battleview Loyal Orange Lodge No. 1972, who conveyed it to the Presbyterian Church. The hum of binders and throb of threshing engines ceased, all business was suspended while the citizens of Lashburn and neighbours from Wycollar attended the funeral. The service, which was held in the Presbyterian Church, was conducted by RW Br Rev George B Cree, DGC, Saskatchewan. In the course of his remarks the reverend gentleman referred to the sorrowing relatives, who lived in far-away Ulster, in the shadow of Divis. On behalf of the relatives he thanked the citizens for their kindness in showing such respect to all that was mortal of a brother Ulsterman. The Orange lodge attended in regalia, and headed the funeral procession to the cemetery, where, after the burial service had been conducted, the last sad rites of the Order for a departed brother were performed by Orangemen. Floral tributes were sent by LOL 1972, citizens of Lashburn, Boy Scouts and other friends.[237]

Ulster emigrants played many happier roles in the course of the annual calendar of the lodges, of course, chief among them on the Twelfth Day. Chad Penny, a descendant of an emigrant family from Windy Gap, Whitehead, recalls family history relating to the fact that some of his ancestors were often to be found riding a white horse at Abernethy, Saskatchewan, to symbolise William of Orange on the day of the Orange parades.[238]

While Orangeism abroad was strongest in Canada, meanwhile, Ulster Protestant settlers found comradeship and fraternity in lodges elsewhere in the world. Close at hand was the United States, and sometimes members of the Order from both jurisdictions would meet together for their parades, as occurred in July 1939 at Watertown, Jefferson County, New York, for example.[239] The strength of Orangeism in the United States owed much to Ulster emigration, particularly, in the 19th century and early 20th century, into the northern

An unidentified Boston Orangeman from an old postcard in the author's collection.

part of the States, and also to emigration from neighbouring Canada during depression years in the early 20th century, many of these latter migrants being also of Ulster stock. Orange lodges even flourished in Boston, often seen as that most Irish-American of cities alongside New York. In the US the diametrically opposed position of Orange and Green would come into play with serious consequences in the latter city, but there was little conflict elsewhere. In 1912, for example, an estimated 10,000 US Orangemen paraded through Philadelphia, some lodges covering 15 miles to enter the city, and the day ended peacefully with sports.[240]

Often reports of Orange events give us no direct information on whether those involved are emigrants or born in the country concerned. However in the case of an account of an annual lodge outing of William A Dunlop LOL 512 in Philadelphia, we can glean from the names involved that Ulster connections clearly exist; among those mentioned are John Cordner, James Dempsey, Robert Foster, John Gamble, Richard Graham, James Kane, Thomas Lawson, Herbert Morrison, Robert McCorkell, Frank Wade, Albert Wright, George Wright, and Joseph Young, the latter being District Master of Prince of Orange District Lodge No 4 in Philadelphia. Other surnames listed are Hewton, Lownes, McNicholl, Rugg, Skelly, Snedden, and Springierth.[241] These and other lodges would make vocal their support of unionist opposition to Home Rule or a united Ireland, particularly during the Third Home Rule period, but also later, as is clear from a resolution issued in 1924 and sent to Lord Craigavon, the Ulster Prime Minister:

The State Grand Orange Lodge of New York, in annual session this day, in the City of Brooklyn, unanimously commends your stand for the territorial integrity of Northern Ireland.

Its signatories included men with surnames such as Scott, Morrow, Nelson, and Kelly.[242] Rev George T Lemon, who was among the names on the resolution, was appointed Supreme Grand Secretary of the Grand Orange Lodge of the United States at Boston in September 1924, and was the grandson of a former rector of Gilford in County Down.[243]

Others were equally prominent within their own areas and lodges. Alex Armstrong, who died in Pittsburgh in 1910 was a former Belfastman, well known in soccer circles in the city and also his new home, where he was captain of Pittsburgh Celtic AFC – perhaps surprisingly. He was prominent in Orange circles in the city, and several Orange and Black lodges took part in his funeral procession – Homeward Guiding Star LOL 95, of which he was Past Master, Mount Carmel RBP 7, of which he was WM at the time of his death, Iron City LOL 46 and the Greater Pittsburgh lodge 1159, as

Rev George T Lemon was a Supreme Grand Secretary of US Orangeism and was the grandson of a rector from Gilford, Co Down.

DERRY ORANGEMAN IN AMERICA.

MR Alexander Downing. P.S. G.T.

Alexander Downing of Maghera, County Londonderry, who became a prominent Orangeman in Philadelphia in the 1900s and was a member of Derry True Blues LOL 52 in the American city.

well as members of the Independent Order of Oddfellows, of which Armstrong was also a member.[244]

Philadelphia was one of the Orange strongholds of the 20th century and among the prominent figures there was Alexander Downing, a native of Maghera, County Londonderry. He had been born in the district of Dreenan in September 1860, claimed descent from Downings who fought for William at the Boyne, and had become a member of LOL 1053 in Londonderry before he was sixteen years of age. Emigrating to the United States in February 1876, he sought out an Orange lodge in his new home, becoming a member of Derry True Blues LOL 52 in Philadelphia. Downing's enthusiasm for the Order had resulted in his helping to form several other lodges in the city and elsewhere in Pennsylvania. He also served as treasurer of lodges in Philadelphia and was elected State Grand Master in 1900. An account of his life published in an article in 1903 tells us that Alexander Downing was a grocer on the corner of Fletcher and Amber streets in the city and was also prominent as a Freemason and in other fraternal bodies, something which was common with other emigrants too.[245] In Chicago in 1911 a flute band was making a name for itself. The Freedom Flute Band was comprised almost entirely of Ulstermen and was attached to Freedom Loyal Orange Lodge 14 in the city. Among those listed in a newspaper photograph were the following whose roots lay in the North of Ireland: AB Trotter, secretary, H Smyth, president, G Robinson, J Smyth, H Cunningham,

RJ Irvine, T Johnston, J Johnston (Belfast), S Wilkinson, instructor (Armagh), C Pritchard (Bangor), T Johnston, T Calvert (Armagh), J Moore (Donaghadee) and J Greer (Lurgan). Most of the band were also members of the Orange Order, it was detailed in a contemporary newspaper article.[246]

In Australia there was similar opportunity for Protestants to seek out those of like-mind in Orange lodges, and although the high point of Orangeism there had probably been reached by 1925 when Frederick Reid JP, Past Grand Master of New South Wales, addressed the Twelfth demonstration in Belfast, he could relate that there were some 1000 lodges dotted across the country. He was applauded when he noted that many Ulstermen were 'Down Under' and "nurturing in their far-off land the traditional characteristic of the people of the province."[247]. Orangeism arrived in Australia, as it did in many areas, in two ways, through military warrants being operated by army regiments and through emigrants. The first lodges included Number 260, whose warrant was taken to Australia with the 17th Leicestershire Regiment, while the first 'native', or perhaps civilian lodge would be as good a term, was formed in April 1845 with 59 members and operated in Sydney until it closed in 1968. When the annual meeting of the Grand Lodge of New South Wales was held in 1873 one Br Alexander was credited with having brought the first warrant to the area.[248] Those who followed the footsteps of such men would find a ready welcome if they produced their travelling certificate from a lodge in Ireland or elsewhere.

Chicago's Freedom Flute Band was composed almost entirely of Ulstermen in 1911, with members from Armagh, Belfast, Bangor, Donaghadee and Lurgan.

William Junkins, leaving Larne Royal Blue Lodge No70 in 1886, was granted a certificate to take with him to Australia, as well as a Holy Bible. Not surprisingly in the circumstances, when the lodge meeting ended and refreshments were drunk, the toast was to "all true Orangemen across the Globe".[249] While William Junkins name would largely be lost to history, others would become prominent in Orange circles, such as Thomas J Beresford of Christchurch, a former Grand Secretary of the Middle Island Grand Lodge in New Zealand, who was a Ballyclare man connected to the well-known Beresford family of Florence Court near Enniskillen.[250]

Proportionally probably very few of the emigrants ever returned to their homeland, but for those of the Orange fraternity there was an obvious pull – the Twelfth of July. Among those who came back for the traditional Ulster demonstration was Robert Houston, a native of Cullybackey. He had emigrated to Australia in 1878, then moved to South Africa, a not uncommon route, it would seem. Houston had settled there prior to the Boer War and lived in Johannesburg, and was a Past Master of Prince of Orange LOL 4 in the city, a member of Pretoria Diamond LOL 1 and Sons of Erin LOL 18 in East London. A former Grand Treasurer of the South African Grand Lodge, he was also involved with the Black Institution, being a WM of Golden City RBP 330 in Johannesburg.[251]

County Antrim man TB Campbell died suddenly while on the way to join his lodge on 12 July 1904, having maintained his interest in the Order at his new home in Cleveland near Johannesburg; a native of Killyglen, near Larne, County Antrim, he was a holder of the King's and Queen's medals and had also been awarded a Distinguished Service Order for conduct in the field. It looks possible that Campbell had been introduced to South Africa through the agency of the Boer War and had decided to settle there.[252]

Information on Orangeism generally in South Africa is sparse, but the indication of one letter from an Ulsterman in Transvaal would suggest that there was a strong Northern Irish element involved; Mr S Boyd, writing of Relief of Derry celebrations at Potchefstroom in 1903 claimed that 90 per cent of those present were "old Belfastmen" like himself.[253] The connection with home was related in rather a novel way when RHH Baird of Belfast received an Orange Lily from the Transvaal that same year, sent by his friend J Caughey of Germiston. It was reported:

> Mr Caughey, in an interesting letter which accompanied the flower, states that it is one of a number of roots of the orange lily given to him by Br Henry Beattie of RBP 120, and was the first to bloom in the district. Mr Caughey intends to distribute the cuttings from the other lillies all over the neighbourhood, and so found a new 'Orange colony'. Mr Caughey will be remembered locally as an extensive merchant and resident of the city for many years. Some little time ago he left for South Africa for the benefit of his

Cullybackey man Robert Houston was an influential figure within the Orange Order in South Africa.

health, which is now very much improved, and he is doing excellently in business.[254]

There were other fraternal bodies which claimed the allegiance of Ulster settlers, the most prominent of them being the Masonic Order, like the Orange Order either taken to or augmented by settlers to other parts of the world. While many thousands would belong to the Masonic Order, few could claim as long-standing a membership as Charles McKewen, who was initiated into Lodge 404 at Ballinderry, County Antrim, in 1776, and was believed, in 1869, when he then lived in Quebec, to be the oldest Freemason in the world.[255]

Among others prominent as emigrant Masons were James K Taylor, a native of Belfast who rose to become Provincial Grand Master of the Masonic Province of Rhodesia in 1931 and had been a foundation member of Ulidia Masonic Lodge in Pietermaritzburg, South Africa, in 1910, later becoming a foundation member of the St Patrick Lodge in Salisbury, Rhodesia.[256] William Currell was a County Antrim emigrant who went to the United States in 1910 and was a successful salesman in Pittsburgh, Pennsylvania. He was Senior Warden of his lodge by 1925 as well as a trustee of Liberty Valley

Council No 50 of Royal and Select Master Masons, a Knight Templar, and a member of the administrative council of the Order of De Molay, a Masonic youth organisation. His wife was also involved in Female Masonry in the United States.[257] Larne man Robert Davis, who died in Washington in 1901, was a Knight of Pythias in the city and his funeral, like those of other Ulster emigrants who were Freemasons, included Masonic ceremonies.[258]

Somewhat earlier and north of the border, in 1845 a number of Irish Freemasons, who were members of a number of lodges, met in their new home in Toronto at, appropriately enough, the Tyrone Inn and decided to apply for a warrant of their own. The resultant lodge, probably the first in the city but certainly among the earliest, was known as King Solomon's Lodge of Toronto, and the first Worshipful Master of the lodge was one William Cassidy, whose brother, Solomon, was to be the first secretary.[259] Similarly Ulster emigrants were prominent in early Masonic lodges in Australia. John Hope, a native of Londonderry, and William James Crawford, a Belfast Freemason and a bank manager, were prominent in early Masonic history in South Australia, for example.[260] County Tyrone emigrants to New Zealand founded Masonic Lodge 462 at Tauranga in the Bay of Plenty in 1876, and one historian has noted that the lodge was the first and perhaps only one in the colony whose founders included a good proportion of Irish Freemasons just recently arrived from their native land.[261] Other lodge names in New Zealand underline the presence of settlers from different parts of Ireland, among them Lodge Abercorn, Lodge Leinster and Lodge Ulster. "Lodge Ulster, No 475, was founded in 1875 at Petone, a then small industrial suburb seven miles from Wellington, in and near which there are now more than sixty thousand people; Ulster is the pioneer and leader of the ten flourishing Lodges of the New Zealand Constitution now working among them", according to Masonic history.[262]

There were other fraternal organisations which attracted Protestants, among them was the International Order of Good Templars, a temperance body which attracted large numbers of adherents in the latter 19th century and early years of the 20th century. Although commanding considerable numbers in its heyday, it was never as strong or as enduring as bodies such as the Orange or Masonic Orders. There are occasional historical references to Good Templars leaving their native land and being made the focus for social events. In the County Antrim town of Whitehead in 1902, for example, Shamrock Lodge of the IOGT held a special meeting in their lodgeroom to pay tribute to one J Dick, who was bound for South Africa. He was probably related to the Samuel Dick, who also emigrated from Whitehead to South Africa that December and who was presented with a Gold Albert and Seal by his colleagues in a local building firm.[263] Given the two men's apparent 'working class' backgrounds, history unfortunately records very little

about them or their future lives in the land of their adoption. As far as the Good Templars went, however, it was likely that someone like Dick might try to link up with brethren in his new homeland, but numbers might have been less impressive than at home. This does not appear to have been the case in New Zealand in the 1870s, however, where it was recorded that a local electoral candidate for Invercargill, Sutherland, had won the contest ". . . by means of the votes of the Society of Good Templars in the town."[264]

Fraternities were important means, depending on their respective strengths, in helping provide a grounding for new emigrants into the area which they were hoping to settle and find employment. In the Canadian example, Orange lodges were dotted across many areas such as Alberta, Ontario, Newfoundland and Saskatchewan, making it very easy to make contacts which provided not only a social base but also the potential for assistance in finding employment. It was said, for example, that an Ulsterman or women seeking employment with Eaton's in Canada was assured of a job if they worked well, and that if they were an Orangeman their prospects were even greater. The Orange and Green did not always mix well in new lands, and in the United States there was often conflict between the two in the 19th century. The example of Boston is an interesting one, where dominance of the Roman Catholic Irish resulted in the small community of Protestant Irish forming themselves into a separate fraternal grouping, the Irish Protestant Mutual Relief Society, for example,[265] and one author noted of the Roman Catholic Bostonians that ". . . though they distrusted live Orangemen, the Irish made the dead Scotch-Irish their own"[266]

There were a surprising number of live Orangemen, even in places such as Boston, where a Twelfth parade attracted considerable numbers up until at least the 1930s. An account of the 1930 event, which saw a parade through the streets from Coply Park to South Station, noted 45 lodges, bands and ladies lodges of the Orange Order, and Royal Black Preceptory having taken part. They then boarded buses for a social day held at Mayflower Grove, also holding an evening meeting and a concert by one of the lodge pipe bands.[267] A few years later one of the most unusual events associated with Protestant fraternities overseas took place on a liner, the SS *California*, which was bringing American Orangemen across the Atlantic to Belfast for the Twelfth demonstration. It was reported that a lodgeroom was created in the table tennis room of the ship, a programme having been produced for the occasion by the ship's printer. Among those who took part in the event were a large number of Ulster-born exiles, among them the Worshipful Master for the event, John Berryman (Philadelphia), a native of Moneymore in County Londonderry, with James Scott (Philadelphia), originally from Omagh, as his deputy. Newtownards exile James A Watson, also from Philadelphia, was Master of Ceremonies,

Ulster's Roman Catholic emigrants to the USA could maintain links with home through organisations such as the Ancient Order of Hibernians, founded in the United States in 1836 although it was not incorporated until 1853, when it took part in its first St. Patrick's Day parade. This certificate was printed in Boston, one of the heartlands of Irish-American settlement.

and another from the city, John Condor, originally from Portadown, was Chaplain. A New York Orangeman, Ian Hunter, who was from Londonderry, was Secretary, while others listed in reports of the event include Joseph Scott (originally from Letterkenny, County Donegal), Robert Jamison and James Nichol (Coleraine), John Puess, RJ Crow, Samuel Wilson and William Patterson (Belfast) and John Logan (Dundalk).[268]

The event reminds one of an old photograph seen once, and taken in the middle of the wheatfields in Saskatchewan, Canada. At a crossroads, standing in front of the general store, and with nothing but wheat for miles, was a group of men. On closer inspection, you could see that they had a banner with them and were standing in formation; it was the Twelfth parade in a far off land, a long way from the field at Edenderry.

[228] Quoted in the *Larne Times* and *Weekly Telegraph* of 18 July 1925

[229] Houston and Smyth, *The Sash Canada Wore, A Historical Geography of the Orange Order in Canada*, Toronto, 1980, is an excellent and well-researched account of Orangeism in British North America

[230] *Larne Reporter* 16 January 1886, additional information including a copy of the Travelling Certificate from the Canadian archives by Marnie Thompson, Vancouver, Canada

[231] *The Dominion Illustrated* account (detailed in the *Larne Reporter*, 3 May 1890)

[232] Bruce S Elliott, *Irish Migrants in the Canadas A New Approach*, Kingston and Montreal, 1988

[233] a detailed documentary history, for example, is provided by RS Pennefather, *The Orange and the Black, Documents in the history of the Orange Order, Ontario and the West 1890–1940*, Canada, 1984

[234] Gary Dennis, *The Spirit of the Twelfth*, Gravenhurst, Ontario, 1982

[235] Dennis, op cit, p32

[236] *Larne Times* and *Weekly Telegraph*, 14 April 1906

[237] *Weekly Telegraph*, 29 September 1918

[238] Interview with Chad Penny during a visit to County Antrim, 31 May 2001

[239] Article in the *Watertown Daily Times*, New York, Wednesday 12 July 1939. I am grateful to Brian McConnell, Orange historian in Nova Scotia, for supplying this article.

[240] *Weekly Telegraph*, 3 August 1912

[241] *Weekly Telegraph*, 4 November 1939

[242] *Weekly Telegraph*, 5 July 1924

[243] ibid., 20 September 1924

[244] *Weekly Telegraph*, 26 February 1910

[245] *Weekly Telegraph*, 20 June 1903

[246] *Weekly Telegraph*, 21 January 1911

[247] *Weekly Telegraph*, 18 July 1925

[248] *Belfast News Letter*, 29 May 1873

[249] *Larne Times*, 25 September 1886

[250] *Weekly Telegraph*, 28 September 1901

[251] *Weekly Telegraph*, 17 June 1933

[252] *Larne Times*, 13 August 1904

[253] *Weekly Telegraph*, 26 September 1903

[254] *Weekly Telegraph*, 28 March 1903

[255] *Belfast News Letter*, 8 November 1869

[256] *Weekly Telegraph*, 21 February 1931

[257] *Weekly Telegraph*, 1 August 1925

[258] *Larne Times*, 23 March 1901

[259] see 'A Link with Canadian Masonry' in *Masonic Grand Lodge of Research, Transactions 1963–1968, Vol XV*, 1970

[260] see James H Weir, 'Early Irish Freemasonry in South Australia', *Grand Masonic Lodge of Ireland Lodge of Research*, Belfast, March 1986

[261] see 'Irish Freemasonry in New Zealand', *Masonic Lodge of Research Transactions for the years 1949–1957*, Dublin, 1959

[262] ibid., p116–7

[263] *Larne Times*, 13 December 1902; 20 December 1902

[264] *Belfast News Letter*, 16 October 1851

[265] Oscar Handlin, *Boston's Immigrants. A Study in Acculturation*, New York, 1974, p163

[266] Handlin, p145

[267] *Weekly Telegraph*, 2 August 1930

[268] *Weekly Telegraph*, 20 July 1935

'Kentucky Rifles': Ulstermen and their descendants on the battlefield

A re-enactor at Elijah Clarke State Park in Georgia steps back into the 18th century, a time when many Ulster-Scots settlers shouldered their muskets in Indian Wars and the American Revolution.

In his poem about the American Revolution, *Hi Uncle Sam*, Tyrone cleric and poet WF Marshall expresses the view that "Whenever there was fighting, or wrong that needed righting, an Ulsterman was sighting his Kentucky gun with care" and there can be little doubt that men from this part of the world have played a prominent part in regimental conflicts and military history. Some of the emigrants or their descendants were famous soldiers – Stonewall Jackson and Ulysses Simpson Grant in the American Civil War, for example; others were not so famous.

Joseph McLernon falls into this latter category. Born in County Antrim, he lies buried in the wild and now peaceful mountains of Central Arizona, where he died during a battle with Apache Indians in 1882. McLernon was a US Cavalryman and he and other men of Troop E, Sixth Cavalry, were sent there to quell Native American unrest. They were to be based at Fort Apache, and soon found themselves in a situation of increasing unrest, with the Tonto and Cibecue Apaches in conflict with the authorities and settlers

It was a far cry from a more peaceful life in County Antrim, where McLernon had been born in November 1858. Little is known about him – not even the town or place of his birth – but when he arrived in America in 1880 the emigrant said he had been a labourer, and he most probably had experience on a farm and with horses.

Two other Irish emigrants, Frank McGee and Auburn McKenna also joined the US army within the next few days in Baltimore, and historians believe they may have all come to America on the same boat. The other two were posted to different units, McLernon to Arizona. Initially he was involved in routine patrols and work – repairing telegraph lines on one occasion, for example. But there were skirmishes and battles, showing that the Indians were formidable opponents. As a band of around 100 renegade Apaches rampaged through the area of East Clear Creek in July 1882, the Sixth Cavalry was sent to search them out. The Indian band had already burned homes, stolen cattle and horses and killed a number of people.

In a pine-forest the US soldiers, who had been following a party of Indians to their camp, were engaged by a large group of Apaches. In the skirmish which followed McLernon was shot in the arm, but the bullet also proved fatal, smashing one of his ribs and passing through both lungs. Despite considerable personal danger, Lieutenant Thomas Cruse, who had been with Private McLernon, dragged him to a safe position. As he and Captain John Horan made the Antrim exile more comfortable, the Indians took the opportunity of nightfall to slip away from their pursuers.

Captain Adna Chaffe would later send a report to his headquarters about the aftermath of the battle, in which he stated:

> Troops E and I gathered up the wounded of the line occupied by them – Lt Morgan, Sgt Conn, and Private McLernan (sic) and took them bodily to camp across the Big Dry Fork. The wounded suffered severely while being carried across the canyon, but the men conveyed them with all possible care. They often fell and let the wounded fall. The task was the most difficult kind, but was accomplished by 10.30pm. Private McLernon died forty minutes after we reached camp. Captain Abbot was unable to carry off his wounded and they remained on the north side of the canyon during the night.

Joseph McLernon was wrapped in a blanket and buried in a shallow grave, his grave site being marked by stones at the remote location. Gone and almost forgotten, Joseph McLernon's last resting place was known to a few forest rangers and history enthusiasts. It was forest ranger Fred W Croxen who campaigned for a gravestone for the young County Antrim soldier and in July 1976 a military marker stone was unveiled at the grave, in a ceremony attended by 28 enthusiasts and addressed by a professor from the Northern Arizona University.

Although some historical controversy surrounded whether the site was the actual grave site or McLernon's body was later exhumed and buried at Fort Apache, Stanley C Brown argues convincingly in *The Journal of Arizona History* (Spring 1998) that:

> . . . the body of Joseph McLernon rests in the beautiful and peaceful wilds of Arizona's central mountains, and the marker erected there is one thing appreciative citizens could do for the sacrifice he made.

It is a fitting way to remember the life and unfortunate death of a 23 year-old emigrant from County Antrim – Cavalryman Joseph McLernon, Troop E, Sixth Cavalry, late of Fort Apache.[269]

The Reilly family of Limavady, who emigrated to Wellington, Ontario, in the 1920s, would provide a major military footnote in the Second World War as far as Canadian military history is concerned. Amazingly, the family sent nine brothers, all in the same regiment, off to war in Europe, the oldest of them 41 years and the youngest 22. The brothers were all members of the local militia before the outbreak of the war and all subsequently volunteered for active service. They were the sons of Samuel Reilly, formerly of Main Street, Limavady, and during the war some of them would return to their native land, being feted by, among others, the Lord Mayor of Belfast, and the Moderator of the General Assembly of the Presbyterian Church in Ireland. While Irish America might provide 'the Fighting Sullivans' – about whom a wartime movie was made – the Ulster-Scots certainly bettered the record of service with their nine 'Fighting Reillys'.[270] They were also a formidable group, if the comment from Corporal William H Reilly to one Northern Ireland newspaper was anything to go by:

> We're Ulstermen, and we're proud to be in this fight. We are known as the 'Fighting Reillys' and anyone who interferes with one of us must deal with the lot.

In the First World War, Ulster was keen to claim a Canadian officer as its own, after he was awarded the Victoria Cross posthumously. The *Weekly Telegraph* informed readers in April 1916 that Belfast's first VC of the war was the late Company Sergeant Major Frederick William Hall, of the 8th Battalion, Canadian Infantry. His mother had been born in Belfast and was a daughter of Thomas Finn of Atlantic Avenue on the Antrim Road, while his aunt, Mrs Nichol, lived at Hopefield Avenue in the city. Hall had spent part of his boyhood in Belfast, and lived for a time with his aunt in the city. He was in Winnipeg in Canada when the war broke out and joined the 90th Winnipeg Rifles. He came to Europe as a private with the 8th Battalion of the Canadian Expeditionary Force and gained rapid promotion. The Belfast man received the Victoria Cross for his efforts at Ypres in Belgium in May 1915 to rescue a wounded man who had fallen just 15 yards from the Canadian trench; he had been mortally wounded on the second attempt to bring the man back to safety.[271]

In the Second World War many soldiers of Ulster origin and descent fought in battlefields across the world. Among them was Private John J Hamill of Chicago, Illinois, in the

USA, who had been born at Mullaghsandal in the Glens of Antrim. He had lived in the United States since the age of eight years, and in the Second World War served with the 82nd Airborne Division, seeing action in North Africa, Sicily, Italy, France and Germany. Hamill fought in Normandy despite a broken jaw and several wounds, and his condition was only ascertained after he was struck by a falling tree and taken for medical attention. A hotel employee in civilian life, he took the opportunity while in Europe and on leave to visit his aunt Mrs Ellen Magill in County Antrim and would later earn a footnote in history back across the Atlantic when he became the 100,000th US soldier to be demobilised after the war.[272]

In other conflicts Ulster exiles proved valiant fighters, and nowhere so than in the American Revolution, where the first shots fired in anger were said to have been fired from Scotch-Irish muskets on the Alamance River of North Carolina.[273] During the Revolution Ulster settlers played a major role in the Revolutionary cause, and George Washington was moved to make a famous speech that if defeated elsewhere his last stand for liberty would be among the Scotch-Irish of his native Virginia. In some areas the Ulster settlers did not take a significant part in the struggle until the war came to them with a vengeance; this happened, for example, in the Waxhaws Region of the Carolinas, where a massacre of Virginian and other troops by the infamous Green Dragoons unit of the British Army took place. Locals nursed wounded Americans in the nearby Waxhaw Presbyterian Church, which was burned down by the troops as a consequence, among the nurses involved was Elizabeth Jackson, mother of the future President, Andrew Jackson. The Jacksons, of course, provide a sobering example of the total commitment of many Ulster families to the Patriot cause during the Revolution. Andrew lost his two brothers during the conflict, one of them dying of fatigue, another of smallpox, while his mother died of a fever in the port of Charles Town while nursing wounded Americans on a prison ship.[274] Once committed to the cause, the Ulster settlers proved difficult to contain. When large numbers of 'Over Mountain Men' gathered at Sycamore Shoals in Tennessee prior to marching south to do battle with Major Patrick Ferguson and his force of Loyalists and Redcoats, they were despatched by a fiery preacher believed to have ancestral links with Ballynure. Samuel Doak told those who bowed their heads at Sycamore Shoals in September 1780:

> My countrymen, you are about to set out on an expedition which is full of hardships and dangers, but in which the Almighty will attend you.

The Over Mountain Men, many of them first generation Ulster settlers, crossed the Smoky Mountains to do battle with British forces at Kings Mountain during the Revolutionary War. Fiery County Antrim cleric Samuel Doak sent them off with a rousing speech and prayer and they proved victorious against Major Patrick Ferguson and his men.

The Mother Country has her hands upon you, these American Colonies, and takes that for which our fathers planted their homes in the wilderness – OUR LIBERTY. Taxation without representation and the quartering of soldiers in the homes of our people without their consent are evidence that the Crown of England would take from its American Subjects the last vestige of Freedom. Your brethren across the mountains are crying like Macedonia unto your help. God forbid that you shall refuse to hear and answer their call – but the call of your brethren is not all. The enemy is marching hither to destroy your homes.

Brave men, you are not unacquainted with battle. Your hands have already been taught to war and your fingers to fight. You have wrested these beautiful valleys of the Holston and Watauga from the savage hand. Will you tarry now until the other enemy carries fire and sword to your very doors? No, it shall not be. Go forth then in the strength of your manhood to the aid of your brethren, the defence of your liberty and the protection of your homes. And may the God of Justice be with you and give you victory.

Let Us Pray

Almighty and gracious God! Thou hast been the refuge and strength of Thy people in all ages. In time of sorest need we have learned to come to Thee – our Rock and our Fortress. Thou knowest the dangers and snares that surround us on march and in baffle. Thou knowest the dangers that constantly threaten the humble, but well beloved homes, which Thy servants have left behind them. O, in Thine infinite mercy, save us from the cruel hand of the savage, and of the tyrant. Save the unprotected homes while fathers and husbands and sons are far away fighting for freedom and helping the oppressed. Thou, who promised to protect the sparrow in its flight, keep ceaseless watch, by day and by night, over our loved ones. The helpless woman and little children, we commit to Thy care. Thou wilt not leave them or forsake them in times of loneliness and anxiety and terror. O God of Battle, arise in Thy might. Avenge the slaughter of Thy people. Confound those who plot for our destruction. Crown this mighty effort with victory, and smite those who exalt themselves against liberty and justice and truth. Help us as good soldiers to wield the Sword of The Lord and Gideon. Amen[275]

The outcome of the battles of Kings Mountain and Hanna's Cowpens, both in South Carolina, was that the King's troops were defeated. The British policy had been to defeat the rebels in the southern colonies and encourage those loyal to the King to flock into militia units, then move against Washington and the Continental Army in the north. The result of the battles made it impossible for this to happen, and the term 'Hornet's Nest' which was applied originally to the area around Mecklenburg County and Charlotte, could as easily have been applied to the entire Carolinas.

On the memorial at Kings Mountain the names of American soldiers killed there shows a clear predominance

This statue in the city of Spartanburg, South Carolina, commemorates Draperstown's General Daniel Morgan, victor of the Battle of Cowpens and one of many Ulstermen who helped lead the American cause in the Revolutionary War.

of Ulster surnames, and some were, in fact, only arrived after 1772 from Ballymena, Ballymoney and elsewhere.[276] One among many of the soldiers who fought at the Cowpens was James Carlisle, born in May 1763 in County Monaghan, who served under his brother Lieutenant Francis Carlisle, and Colonel Andrew Pickens, another Ulster-Scot. The 1781 battle saw Carlisle and the others under the overall command of General Daniel Morgan, whose roots are believed to lie in Draperstown in County Londonderry.[277] Among those from the Ulster counties known to have fought in one or both of the two major battles were:

● Arthur Erwin, who was born in County Antrim in March 1738 and was the son of Nathaniel Erwin. He went to America with his parents and the family settled in Bucks County, Pennsylvania, later moving to North Carolina. He married a Margaret Brandon and survived the Revolutionary war, dying in August 1821.

● Colonel James Hawthorne, was born in 1750 in Armagh and settled on the frontiers of South Carolina, where he was captured by Indians, along with his mother and two sisters when he was around 12 years old. He later served in Indian wars and with the militia. In addition to the Battle of Kings Mountain, he took part in several other battles and skirmishes, and was wounded at the Battle of the Cowpens in January 1781. He married Mary Neel and the couple had four children. The County Armagh man died in 1809 in Kentucky.

● Captain Patrick Carr, a native of County Londonderry, had settled in Georgia when the Revolutionary war broke out. He served under Colonel Elijah Clarke, another Ulster-Scot, taking part in actions in the colony before moving into the mountains of the Carolinas after they fell to the British, subsequently taking part in the Battle of Kings Mountain. He was promoted to Major and was said to be a major scourge to the Tories – those Americans loyal to the King – supposedly having killed around 100 of them in the conflict. He was murdered in 1802 in Jefferson County, Georgia, possibly by someone settling an old score from the Revolutionary War.

There were also many others who are listed as having been natives of Ireland. In the context of their surnames and the communities from which they were coming, the majority of these were undoubtedly part of the Presbyterian migration from Ulster to America.

Not all those who took part in the American Revolution were on the Revolutionary side. There were many colonists who remained loyal, either publicly or privately, to the King. One of those who very publicly supported the ties with Great Britain – and who paid the price for doing so – was a Ballymena man named Alexander Chesney. He was born in the townland of Dunclug near Ballymena in September 1755 and died at his home, Packolet, outside Kilkeel, County Down, in January 1845. Chesney was one of those whose story historians have begun to tell more often in recent times – those American settlers who remained loyal to the Crown during the Revolution. Ironically, while Chesney was fighting with the Royalist side at Kings Mountain in South Carolina, fellow countrymen from Ballymena were engaged in his defeat. The Hodge family, to whom the Chesneys were related through marriage, was fighting on the side of the American rebels, as were another related family, the Colemans. The latter changed sides, like Alexander Chesney, and switched to the loyalist side, but the Hodges remained on the American (and ultimately the winning) side[278]

Liam Kelly JP, DL, the chairman of Larne Ulster American Committee, lays a wreath at Kings Mountain in honour of those from Ulster who fought in the 1780 battle there during the American Revolution. The wreath laying took place in 1998 when a delegation from Larne visited Clover as part of a twinning arrangement between the two areas.

Alexander Chesney was the son of a County Antrim farmer called Robert Chesney (or McChesney), who farmed first at Dunclug, then at Kirkinriola a short distance away. He and his family sailed from Larne on the vessel *James and Mary* in August 1772, bound for Charles Town, South Carolina. On a vacant tract of 400 acres of land near the Pacolet river, which lay around 250 miles to the north, the Chesney's settled and made their new home.

Within a few years, the American Revolution came about, and Alexander Chesney's journal reveals that at an early stage he was helping Loyalists to evade the Patriots by guiding them into North Carolina to government troops. He had an early indication of how such actions were viewed by the American forces when his house was ransacked and he was taken prisoner and forced to join their number. Chesney saw service against the Indians and took part in actions in Georgia and East Florida before the fall of Charles Town to the British gave him his opportunity to seek 'protection', promising to desist from action against the King and joining the Loyalist militia.

His first action was at Bullock Creek, an area settled by many from Ulster, as is evidenced by the Presbyterian Church located there, and was successful. That Chesney displayed great courage during this time is evident from his excursion into the Patriot camp at Cherokee Ford, where he counted the tents and wagons, discovered the names of the leaders and ascertained the whereabouts of 500 horsemen who had gone to attack a nearby fort. He was captured after leaving the camp, but managed to make good an escape a short time afterwards.

In August 1780 the Ballymena man was appointed Captain and Assistant Adjutant General under Major Patrick Ferguson, and the force which the Aberdeen-born officer mustered (the bulk of it American loyalist) enjoyed some successes in routing the rebels. But far away in Tennessee, the 'Over Mountain Men' were mustering, responding to threats from Ferguson about laying down their weapons by marching to meet him. When they approached him after their long march over the mountains and Ferguson heard the numbers they boasted, he decided to seek a defensive position on the hilltop called Kings Mountain. The Americans were expert shots and they would use the tree cover to good advantage to pick off their opponents, as Chesney recounted in his journal:

> Kings Mountain from its height would have enabled us to oppose a superior force with advantage, had it not been covered with wood which sheltered the Americans and enabled them to fight in the favourite manner...they were able to advance in three divisions under separate leaders to the crest of the hill in perfect safety until they took the post and opened an irregular but destructive fire from behind trees and other cover.

His account details the disaster that befell Ferguson and his force; the commander was killed, one-third of his force wiped out and many, including Alexander Chesney, were wounded.

Congress ordered a medal to be struck to commemorate the victory of the American forces at Cowpens under the command of General Daniel Morgan, whose roots lay in Draperstown, County Londonderry. Morgan's victory in January 1781 helped spell the end of British hopes to capture the southern states and thus helped lead to the surrender of Cornwallis at Yorktown.

Chesney was taken as a prisoner following the battle and witnessed a trial and hanging of ten of the loyalists who were captured. He refused to join the Patriots and was assured that he would be among those executed if he did not. The prisoner managed to evade his captors while being marched with others away from the approaching forces of Tarleton, an officer whose ruthlessness spread fear among the rebel militia units. He was recaptured and paroled but saw further service with the King's troops, witnessing a second major defeat, at Hanna's Cowpens.

"We suffered a total defeat by some dreadful bad management", Chesney records of the Battle of the Cowpens. It was a defeat which helped bring about the eventual end of the war, for the British command now realised that the south could not be subdued. For Americans it was the beginning of victory and freedom.

For those such as Alexander Chesney, however, it was the beginning of the end. Many of them lost their lands and homes. Chesney himself appears not to have had his land confiscated in the aftermath of the war, the state simply regarding it as having been abandoned and then re-granting it. Either way, the outcome was the same. Alexander Chesney had by this stage headed back across the Atlantic, leaving behind also the sorrow of his wife having died in the Carolinas and his young son having been sent to his mother in the 'Back country' to be looked after.

A new chapter in Chesney's life would open, with his appointment as a Revenue Inspector in Ireland. It was

Above: The ridge at Kings Mountain, where Ulster militiamen from North Antrim stormed the British positions. The monument there was placed by families of those who took part in the 1780 battle.

Left: The grave of Alexander Chesney in Kilkeel. Originally from Ballymena, he served in the Loyalist forces during the American Revolution and later returned to Northern Ireland, obtaining a position as a Customs official. Chesney died in 1845 in his 88th year.

this role which would bring him within a short time to Kilkeel, County Down, where the view of the sea was clear from the home he built and named Packolet after the river in South Carolina where the family had once settled. In 1797 Alexander Chesney would again put his American military experience to good use through the raising of a company, known as the Mourne Infantry, to try and prevent disturbances associated with the United Irishmen. Once again in this entry we have the sense of old adversaries meeting again; Chesney was challenging men who were greatly influenced by the American victory in the Revolutionary War.

Alexander Chesney died in 1845, in his 88th year, and is buried in the Mourne Presbyterian Church cemetery in Kilkeel. His memorial states that he held seven commissions under the British Crown and that:

> . . . the duties of his public life were varied and difficult and in the discharge of them he ever maintained an upright character and a conduct at once faithful and exemplary . . . And, although when a Captain in the American War he lost his earthly possessions yet God, manifested in the flesh in whom he firmly trusted, never forsook him but blest him abundantly even in temporal things.

The Revolution, as the Chesney example helps to illustrate, was a civil war between families and communities in many areas. But in another major schism in America life, in the 1861–1865 War Between the States, the evidence for the division was accorded the actual title of a civil war.

Again, Ulstermen, or their descendants, were found to be among the forces on both sides. Indeed, there was at least one Ulsterman who took part in the battle which started the American Civil War, Private John Thompson of Articlave, County Londonderry. He was serving in the 1st US Artillery and was inside the garrison at Fort Sumter in South Carolina when it was fired upon by Confederate forces, thus starting the Civil War. John wrote home to his father Robert Thompson in Articlave to allay any concerns which he would undoubtedly have had about his son:

> My Dear Father, Your letter dated January 11th has been dearly received, and I am exceedingly glad to hear of your welfare. You are anxious you say in your letter to know all about the war, or properly speaking the rebellion of South Carolina. Ever since the election of President (sic) in November last great dissatisfaction has prevailed in the Slave States, and during December this State formally seceded from the Union, and openly threatened to take forcible possession of the Forts, Arsenals and other public property in this harbour. This they were certain could be easily accomplished, as two of the three forts in this harbour were without any garrison and the third, Fort Moultrie being garrisoned by only seventy five United States artillerymen. Certain of success they ingeniously set about warlike preparations, all the time keeping a very strict watch on the helpless little garrison of which I formed a member. Steamboats were nightly set to watch us to prevent our moving to Sumter distant about a mile. On the night of 26 December shortly after sun down, we were formed in heavy marching order, and quietly marched out of Moultrie leaving only a few men behind on Guard, and embarking on board a number of small boats that were in readiness, we safely landed in Sumter. The consternation of the Carolinians may be imagined next morning when they observed Fort Moultrie enveloped in flames and smoke, and at noon saw the Stars and Stripes proudly waving from the battlements of Fort Sumter. During the night of the 26th the men left behind spiked all the guns, and then set fire to the gun carriages, etc, at the abandoned fort and then left it to quietly be taken possession of by troops of South Carolina. This they were not long in doing, they can scale the walls of an unoccupied fort with a gallantry highly commendable . . . Fort Sumter which we now occupy is fine sided brick work, walls from 12 to 15½ feet thick, mounting three tier of guns of the highest calibre, and completely surrounded by water.

Thompson refers to the strengthening of the defences at Sumter and the building of formidable buttresses by the Confederates, and he tells his father:

> You need not be in any unnecessary anxiety on my account, for to tell the truth in spite of all their bluster I am almost sure they never will fire a shot at us.

In a subsequent letter from Fort Hamilton, New York, on 28 April 1861, he tells how the Confederates cut all communications to Sumter and food supplies ran low:

> We had been on three-quarters rations for a long time and on 8 April a reduction to half rations was made and cheerfully submitted to . . . on the eleventh one biscuit was our allowance, and matters seemed rapidly coming to a crisis.

Thompson account details, adding that on 13 April at 4.30am the first shell was fired at the fort and burst above their heads. The Sumter batteries opened fire at 6.30am and the firing would continue relentlessly for four hours. Damage to the fort was considerable, although there were no casualties. Thompson gives an account in which the Union forces dictated their terms of surrender to the South Carolina forces:

> Thus ended the fight and here I am without a scratch, no one being wounded in the fight but the man above alluded to. I forgot to mention that during the fire on the second day our flag was shot down, but it only remained down a few moments when it again floated from our ramparts, nailed with temporary nails to a new stick.

The conflict would see many such actions, most of them with rather more serious and severe casualties than Thompson witnessed in April 1861.[279] Another Ulsterman in the Union forces was Colonel Thomas M Reid of New York, the fourth son of Thomas Reid of Culmore, near Londonderry, and no doubt the actions at Fort Sumter

A Civil War re-enactor dresses in the authentic uniform of a Confederate soldier in Greenville, South Carolina.

would be of some significance to them, having come from a region where a besieged city formed an important part of the historical landscape.[280]

The British Empire saw many local men enlisting for army service and ending up in various parts of the world. The British Army saw conflict in far flung corners of the world, requiring the despatch of soldiers to quell rebellions or internecine strife as was the case in India, for example, where General John Nicholson became prominent for his valour, and South Africa where many regular and volunteer soldiers fought against the Boers. In 1900, as the war continued in South Africa, former Ballymena man JD Blakely, watched from the sidelines in Montreal in Canada. He had volunteered for service, but been turned down on account of his age (an army pensioner, he had first seen action during the Crimean War at the Battle of Alma in September, 1854). Blakely, had been a colour sergeant with Princess Victoria's Royal Irish Fusiliers in Montreal, and he took the opportunity to write to the *Weekly Telegraph* newspaper in Belfast to

highlight his support for the first Canadian contingent that had been sent to South Africa.[281]

Blakely also provided an account of his service during the Crimean War, outlining that at one point, as they were crossing a river one of his colleagues in the 7th Royal Fusiliers shouted out "Just imagine you are crossing the Boyne." The old soldier recalled how his unit had charged into the Russian lines, eventually capturing several of their cannon. He concluded an extensive article by highlighting his service:

I served with the 7th at the Battle of Inkerman, and in January 1855, I was transferred to the 69th Regiment, now the 2nd Royal Irish Fusiliers, being claimed by an elder brother in that regiment. I served with the 69th throughout the Crimean War and afterwards in the Cape of Good Hope and the Indian mutiny and left it in India on the expiration of my first term of service (10 years). Three of my brothers and myself served in the 89th and one in the Royal Marines. That was five out of seven of us that gave our services to our beloved Queen.

Right: A Confederate memorial in Richburg, South Carolina, contains many Ulster-Scots surnames, signifying the impact the American Civil War had on the tightly-knit communities of the southern states in particular.

Below: The Confederate Memorial in the city of Greenville, South Carolina. Most towns and cities in the state have such memorials in town centres of other locations.

Samuel Delaney (right) of the New Zealand Expeditionary Force met up with his brother William, then serving in the Royal Artillery, when both were in North Africa during the Second World War. This photograph would be the last which they would have taken together; both were to make the supreme sacrifice.

courtesy The Delaney family, Ballycarry, County Antrim

At the other side of the British Commonwealth, Ulster settlers in Australia and New Zealand also played their part in military efforts. Lieutenant WA Cloughry of Larne joined the 9th Light Horse in his new home in Australia when the First World War broke out, and was wounded twice at Gallipoli, the second necessitating his being invalided from the theatre of conflict and sent to England. There he gained a pilot's licence at Hendon and was in due course appointed a captain and flight commander in charge of an aerodrome. His younger brother was an officer in the Royal Engineers who had seen service at the Battle of the Somme.[282]

New Zealanders included Private Samuel Delaney of the New Zealand Expeditionary Force in the Second World War. Delaney was a native of the village of Ballycarry, County Antrim, and an amazing coincidence saw both he and his elder brother William James, who served with the Royal Engineers, in the same area in North Africa during the campaign there. The two Ballycarry brothers held their own reunion in the North African desert and had a photograph taken for their family at home in Northern Ireland. It was a poignant irony that the photo recorded the last time they would meet together; both men were subsequently killed in the North African Campaign.[283]

Military service in some areas, particularly prior to the 20th century, was beset with the same problems as settlement for civilians – climatic adjustment and disease. There were many servicemen who died across the Empire of natural causes, among them Lieutenant Patterson of Dromore, County Down, who was Brigade Major in the colony of Sierra Leone when he died in 1829.[284]

There were also many of Ulster stock who continued to enlist and serve in peacetime. Leading Aircraftman James McManus, a native of Whiteabbey, joined the Royal Canadian Air Force in 1952 and was promoted to Corporal three years later. The son of Charles McManus of Battenberg Street, Belfast, he served from 1943–47 in the Royal Air Force and in 1955 was aircraft control operator at the RCAF station at Namao, Alberta.[285]

As time progressed, it was no longer Kentucky rifles that Ulstermen were shouldering, but the term 'the Fighting Irish' could nevertheless continue to be applied to many from these shores and their descendants, who enjoyed military service as a career or embraced it as a service in time of war.

[269] The information on Joseph McLernon comes from Stanley C Brown, 'Whatever happened to Joseph McLernon, killed at the Battle of the Big Dry Wash?', in the *Journal of Arizona History*, Tucson, Spring 1998

[270] *Northern Whig*, 11 January 1940

[271] *Weekly Telegraph*, 1 April 1916

[272] *Larne Times*, 31 January 1946

[273] Rory Fitzpatrick, *God's Frontiersmen*, London, 1989, p102

[274] Robert V Remini, *Andrew Jackson, Volume One, The Course of American Empire, 1767–1821*, New York, 1998, pps 24–25

[275] Doak's fiery sermon and prayer are reprinted in Pat Alderman, *The Overmountain Men*, Tennessee, 1986, p83

[276] Professor Bobby Gilmer Moss, in his excellent book *The Patriots at Kings Mountain*, South Carolina, 1990, provides a complete listing of the Americans who fought on the Revolutionary side at Kings Mountain and their origins

[277] Morgan was elusive about his ancestry according to Don Higginbottom in *Daniel Morgan, Revolutionary Rifleman*, North Carolina, 1961, but Billy Kennedy in his study *The Making of America, How the Scots-Irish Shaped a Nation*, Belfast, 2001, points out that Morgan was a Presbyterian elder, while the presence of the Welsh-sounding name need not be a barrier to the Draperstown claim since there was a Welsh settlement in Donegal during the Ulster Plantation and John James, one of the founders of Williamsburg Presbyterian Church in South Carolina, was a Welsh army officer who had come to Ireland with the Williamite army in the 1690s.

[278] BG Moss, *Journal of Capt Alexander Chesney*, South Carolina, 2002

[279] Private John Thompson's letter to his father Robert, Articlave, County Londonderry, Public Record Office of Northern Ireland, T1585

[280] Belfast Newsletter, 18 October 1869, carries a brief account of Thomas Reid's death in New York at the age of 38.

[281] *Weekly Telegraph*, 22 September 1900

[282] *Larne Times*, 20 January 1917

[283] My thanks to the Delaney family of Ballycarry for providing the information on William James and Samuel

[284] *Belfast News Letter*, 1 September 1829

[285] *Larne Times*, 3 November 1955; he was married to Ellie Mae Gauntlet of Regina, Saskatchewan, and had three children – David Charles, Kathleen May and Susan Jean.

Political exiles from the land of their birth

Chapter 10

The memorial stone to John Neilson, a County Antrim exile of the 1798 Rising who became personal architect to President Thomas Jefferson.
Kevin Donleavy

In a quiet corner of a cemetery at Charlottesville in Virginia is a modern headstone commemorating John Neilson, a County Antrim exile who, like many others, fled or was forced into exile following the ill-fated 1798 United Irish Rising in Ireland. Following the Rising, which had hoped to defeat the government and establish a Republic in Ireland, many of those involved were killed, imprisoned, transported or hanged.

Among those affected by the dramatic decade of the 1790s were the Nelson or Neilson family from the small village of Ballycarry in County Antrim. The village itself was a hotbed of support for the United Irishmen – almost exclusively Presbyterian in this part of Ulster – and most of the menfolk appear to have joined the insurgent forces on 7 June 1798, as they marched to the Battle of Antrim.

Three brothers in the family were involved in what was called locally the 'Turn Oot' and all paid a considerable price for their participation. The youngest, William, was just 16 years old and had the role of acting as a messenger, taking

94

A streetname in Ballycarry village, County Antrim, honours William Nelson, a 16 year-old hanged for his part in the 1798 Rising. His brother John was a prominent architect in exile in Virginia, and a personal friend of President Thomas Jefferson.

a horse from the stables of the local landlord in order to ride between groups of the insurgents from neighbouring Islandmagee and Ballycarry. After the defeat of the rebels at Antrim, William was arrested by the authorities and impressed upon to give up the names of those from the village who had taken part in the event. William, however, knew that if he provided the names of his two brothers, Samuel and John, they would be among those confirmed to have taken a role and would face terms of imprisonment, transportation or worse. At the time both were in fact housed in Carrickfergus Gaol in a separate cell from their brother.

In refusing to assist the authorities, William effectively signed his own death warrant. He was court martialed for his part in the rebellion, found guilty and brought back to his home, where he was hanged on a tree outside his widowed mother's door.

In time Willie Nelson would become known as the Ballycarry Martyr and his grave would form part of a heritage trail in his native village.[286] Samuel Nelson would also lose his life, although more indirectly, dying on a ship which was transporting the two brothers away from Belfast in May 1799. The ship was captured by the French who treated the passengers, most of them exiles, with kindness. But it was later recaptured by the English and sent to the West Indies. Tradition states that John somehow managed to escape from the authorities and reached the United States of America.[287]

Of the three brothers, only John (who spelt his surname Neilson, a variant probably based on the dialect of his home village) thus remained and in his life John reached a prominence which was probably the best manner of

addressing those who had taken the lives of his brothers, for in subsequent years he became a successful architect, keeping in contact with his mother and sending her monies at her new home in Islandmagee. But John Neilson was not only a successful architect, he was also a personal friend of President Thomas Jefferson and President James Madison, high company indeed for the Ulster exile.

Much of Neilson's work can be viewed at the University of Virginia, and at Montpellier, the home of President Madison. At the former, he and another Ulsterman, James Dinsmore, were the master builders for President Jefferson and overseers of the construction of the university.

John was born sometime around 1770–1775 and was the eldest son in the Nelson family. Banished for seven years from his homeland after the 1798 Rising, and, as already mentioned, ending up in the United States he became a naturalized US citizen at Philadelphia in 1804.

The story of his family tragedy apparently became known to the wife of President Madison, and it was said that Mrs Madison showed him many acts of kindness on the account of the sympathy which she felt for him. Undoubtedly the Antrim exile was shown favour by both Madison and Jefferson. He was engaged as master carpenter for sections of the University of Virginia including two pavilions, seven dormitories, the Rotunda and the Anatomical Theatre at the site.

Upper Bremo Plantation, built between 1817 and 1820, is regarded as one of Neilson's finest architectural achievements; indeed it has been called the finest Jeffersonian building not designed by Jefferson.

Neilson built his home in the Vinegar Hill area of Charlottesville and a second nearby, which he subsequently sold to his architect colleague James Dinsmore in 1827. Other property which the political exile owned included a country house, called Refuge.[288] It is clear that in addition to designing and building houses, John was also a keen and enthusiastic gardener; in one of President Jefferson's letters he noted that "He is a gardener by nature and extremely attached to it."

During the Christmas season of 1826, John was at Refuge, when he developed what was described as a violent cold. At the same time he received news of his daughter's death, and this appears to have contributed to a decline which ultimately led to his own death in June, 1827. Something of the success which John Neilson made of his life in exile comes from details of the inventory of his estate, which includes information relating to his library, consisting of 248 volumes, among them books on history, travel, botany, mathematics and architecture. His other property included carpentry and gardening tools, drawing and artists instruments, and a camera obscura.

John was buried in Charlottesville, Virginia, where a monument was erected in April 1999 to commemorate a man described as a "United Irishman, political exile, architect at Monticello and the University of Virginia." The memorial also states his birthplace as "Ballycarry, Co. Antrim, Ireland."[289]

Several facts about Neilson suggest that the Ulster connection was not forgotten in his new home. The executor of his Will was Andrew Leitch, member of a Tyrone Presbyterian family who had come to Charlottesville during the 1700s. One of the things which Leitch wrote back to Belfast about was the sending of a 'profile' of John to his mother, and he requested the famed Mary Ann McCracken, with whom he and other exiles would appear to have kept in touch, to assist the carrier of this 'profile', Mrs John Gorman, in getting the item to his mother. A letter has also survived from Leitch to Thomas Neilson, John's nephew, informing him of John's death and also mentioning the likeness which was being sent across the Atlantic. In Leitch's correspondence he also refers to Neilson's sisters Isabella and Sarah and a fourth brother, Jackson. One of his beneficiaries was also his wife Mary, who was living at Loughmourne, Carrickfergus, at the time of her husband's death. It would appear, meanwhile, that John Neilson of Ballycarry was not the only Ulster exile of 1798 who was cultivated by President Thomas Jefferson. Rev John Glendy, Presbyterian minister of Maghera, County Londonderry, was among those who fled on account of their support of the United Irishmen. The *Belfast News Letter* of April 1833 reported that the death of Glendy had occurred in Philadelphia the previous October. The report detailed:

In the unfortunate distraction of 1798 he was obliged to leave his native country. He was first settled in America as Minister at Staunton, in Virginia, and afterwards removed to Baltimore. In the country of his adoption, he was highly esteemed by all classes and could number among his friends and admirers the late President Jefferson, with whom he became early acquainted, and who, till the close of life, uniformly treated him with kindness and attention.[290]

It also stated that for several years Glendy had been one of the clergymen appointed to preach to the Congress of the United States. The former Maghera minister was buried in Baltimore, a large concourse of members of the congregation there being joined by prominent citizens to pay tribute.

Glendy and Neilson were just two of the many who exchanged their homes for exile in the aftermath of 1798, others who formed an emigrant community and worked for Jefferson included Hugh Chisholm, John Gorman and Joseph Antrim, according to historical sources.[291] In a pamphlet produced for the dedication of Neilson's memorial, it was noted that:

John Neilson lived in a small community of Irish expatriates and American-Irish neighbours in Charlottesville. He certainly was a friend to John Patten Emmet, professor at the University of Virginia and nephew of the revolutionary Robert Emmet (executed in 1803), as well as a friend to James Butler, a United exile from the southeast of Ireland who lived some years in this area. Neilson also had both social and business associations with George O'Toole, who is credited with naming the Vinegar Hill section after that 1798 action in Ireland. Neilson is at rest in Maplewood graveyard among the Leitches from Tyrone, the Flannagans, John Kelly, John O'Connor and wife Emilie, Andrew McKee, TH Hayes from Tipperary, and Thomas McManus, among others.[292]

The 1798 debacle produced a small wave of settlers to the United States from Ulster. Among those who made the journey was Robert Adrain, a mathematician, who was born in Carrickfergus in 1775 and fled to America after the Rising; Adrain subsequently became Professor at Pennsylvania University[293]. The radicalism of Presbyterian minister Samuel Brown Wylie, who was born in Moylarg, County Antrim, in 1773, was said to have led to his departure for Philadelphia in 1797, just ahead of the ill-fated Rising.[294] Among the prominent United Irishmen who made a new start across the Atlantic was Rev Thomas Ledlie Birch, who had been minister at Saintfield in County Down and who died on 12 April 1828, at his new home near Washington, Pennsylvania at the age of 74 years.[295] David Bailie Warden, who was training for the Presbyterian ministry when the Rebellion occurred, subsequently sailed from Larne on an emigrant ship to the US because the Presbytery of Bangor would not licence him. In 1815 at the Congress of Vienna it was a great irony of history that Warden was a United States representative and sat opposite the British Foreign Secretary, Lord Castlereagh, the two men having been on opposite sides in County Down

The ancestors of President William McKinley were believed to be among many Ulster Dissenters who were involved in the 1798 Rising, and became political exiles. Most fled to the United States. This old postcard shows the McKinley ancestral home in County Antrim.

in 1798. Chairs from the Congress table can still be viewed at Castlereagh's home, Mount Stewart, outside Greyabbey.[296]

The *Belfast News Letter* noted in January 1853, meanwhile, the death of John Anderson at Cincinnati, United States, the previous month and related that this Irish exile had fled following the 1798 Rising and lived in Cincinnati from 1800. He had been born in 1751 and survived not only the rebellion but also quite considerable old age – being nearly 101 years of age when he passed away.[297]

An account of the 1798 Rising in County Antrim was written by Larne-born Dr James McHenry, who went to the United States in 1817 and subsequently returned to act as US Consul in Londonderry. McHenry was a popular novelist in the United States and his novel *O'Halloran, or the Insurgent Chief* told the story of the '98 Rising as he recalled witnessing it and hearing accounts of it as a child in his native Larne. McHenry shared something in common with James Orr, the weaver Bard of Ballycarry, who had to flee following the Rising. Orr hid out for a time with Henry Joy McCracken and others following the Battle of Antrim, but they were eventually dispersed on McCracken's order to avoid capture (something which he was personally unable to do). James Orr escaped to America on an emigrant ship, and would write an impression of such a voyage in his poem *The Passengers*, the lines of which include the details that:

> Some frae the stern, wi' thoughts o' grief
> Leuk back, their hearts to Airlan[298]

After around a year in the United States, however, James Orr returned to his native land under amnesty. It would be more common for others to journey in the opposite direction, for an unstable political situation at home continued after the 1798 Rising, being followed by Emmet's Revolt in 1803. In 1804, for example, John Nevin of Knoxville, Tennessee, writing to his brother James at Kilmoyle in County Antrim, could relate how a recent arrival from Ireland named Mr Stewart had informed him ". . . that troublesome times are not likely to be over yet."[299]

Although many of the United Irishmen exiles were not so well known as Nelson and Dinsmore in Virginia, several Ulster emigrants, or their descendants reached high political offices in their new homelands. The United States is probably the most prominent and well known case in point; Presidents of Ulster descent begin with the hardy Andrew Jackson and continue with names such as James Knox Polk, James Buchanan, Andrew Johnson, Theodore Roosevelt, and Woodrow Wilson among them. John Caldwell Calhoun, referred to as the Champion of the Old South, and an adversary of General Andrew Jackson in an argument which was to precede the American Civil War, was the grandson of James Caldwell who emigrated from Ulster to Pennsylvania in 1733. When the Civil War broke out in the 1860s, there was no shortage of Ulstermen involved at a senior level.

There were figures such as General John Cabel Breckinridge, whose ancestors were from a rural townland called Ballyrickardbeg, outside Larne. Breckinridge was the

Vice President of the United States when the war broke out, and he was torn between his loyalties. His native state, Kentucky, was also torn, but decided by a majority to remain with the Union. Breckenridge did not, throwing his lot in with the Confederacy under Jefferson Davis, and he would be the last Confederate Secretary of War, fleeing to Mexico and Europe to avoid the authorities. Those Kentuckians who, like Breckenridge, decided to support the south, were formed into a regiment known as 'the orphan brigade' and won a memorable victory at New Market, where Breckenridge was compared favourably to Stonewall Jackson, one of the finest military leaders the South had. One newspaper, the *Richmond Daily Despatch*, claimed "Gen. Breckinridge . . . has proved himself a worthy successor of Jackson", while the next day the *Richmond Enquirer* added that ". . . celerity of movement, as well as vigour of action, did not desert our cause when Stonewall Jackson died".[300] Breckinridge may have been another Stonewall Jackson, but the cause which he had espoused was to be a lost one, and he was forced into exile to evade the Northern authorities after the surrender of the Confederacy. He spent some time in Central America and in

Europe, although he apparently did not visit the homeland of his Covenanter ancestors, later returning home to the United States. As the centenary of the Union approached the former Vice President was asked to deliver a centenary address at the official commemoration of the momentous landmark in his nation's history. Breckenridge died just ahead of doing so, but his participation would have highlighted that north and south were coming together again.

Breckinridge came from Scots Covenanting stock, comprising Scots Lowlanders, fiercely devout and fundamental in their views. In this he shared his strong Presbyterianism with Woodrow Wilson, who was also a son of the manse. Wilson, whose ancestors were from Strabane and who had the Covenanter martyr Margaret Wilson[301] among his ancestral line, has been described as 'a Presbyterian President'.[302]

In countries other than the United States, emigrants also made their mark. John Ballance was one of those from Ulster who became New Zealand Prime ministers. He was born at Ballypitmave, near Glenavy in County Antrim in March 1839, into a comfortably off, but not prosperous, family. His father, Samuel Ballance, was a Protestant tenant

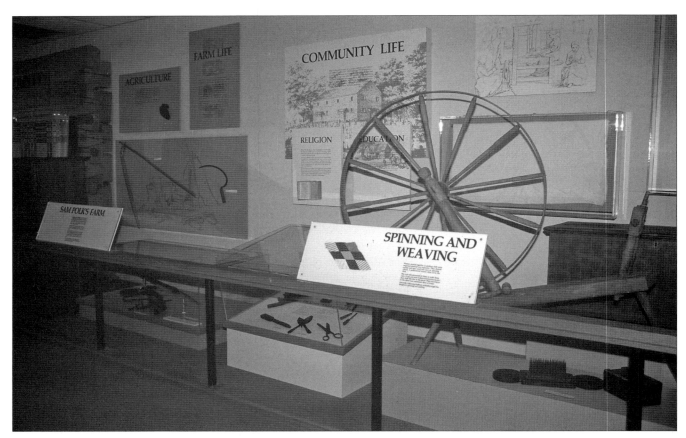

The interior of the Polk Museum in Mecklenburg County, North Carolina. Among the artefacts is a letter to the Polks, whose origins were in Donegal and Londonderry, from Sam Houston, another Ulster-Scots political leader and hero.

President Woodrow Wilson was the son of Presbyterian minister Dr Joseph Ruggles Wilson and the grandson of James Wilson of Dergalt, Strabane, who emigrated to the United States in 1807. The teenage Woodrow Wilson spent four years at this manse in Columbia, South Carolina, between 1870 and 1874, before his father moved to North Carolina to minister there.

farmer 'with evangelical tendencies'; his mother, Mary McNiece, came from a prominent local Quaker family. John was the eldest of a family of eleven children and gained his early education at the local National School, followed by studying at Wilson's Academy in Belfast. His reputation was of a boy who could do nothing but read all day.

Samuel Ballance was active in conservative politics, and at the early age of 16 years his eldest son (John) was helping him to write speeches. The influence of his more liberal mother was also instrumental in shaping John's early political views. At home in Ulster John got a flavour of how divisive politics could be, witnessing a series of major sectarian attacks in Belfast before leaving Wilson's Academy (his education uncompleted) and working for a Belfast hardware firm. In 1857 he left Belfast for Birmingham, where he earned a living as a travelling salesman. He also sought to continue his education by enrolling in evening classes at the Birmingham and Midland Institute, studying politics, biography and history. Birmingham was at the centre of important political and philosophical movements and Ballance took a lively interest in current affairs. He heard speeches by major figures

of the day such as John Bright, Michael Faraday and Joseph Chamberlain, who would become a leader of Liberal Unionists during the Home Rule period in Irish and British history.

The New Zealand connection came through his future wife, Fanny Taylor, the daughter of a licensed victualler; the couple were married at St Peter and St Paul's Church, Aston, in June 1863 and not long afterwards, due in part to Fanny's ill health, they decided to emigrate to New Zealand where she had a brother living. In April 1866 they left London for Melbourne, Australia, and after a short stay continued to New Zealand on a ship called the *Albion*. They arrived at Wellington on 11 August and a few days later travelled on to Wanganui, where Ballance's brother-in-law lived.

Although he made an attempt at a commercial future, opening a shop and selling jewellery he had purchased in Australia, his business was neither successful nor something the County Antrim man contemplated pursuing for long. His chosen career was in journalism and in 1867 he established the *Evening Herald* in partnership with a local printer named AD Willis. Ballance proved to be an able and innovative journalist and managed and edited the *Evening Herald* (from

1876 the *Wanganui Herald)* and its weekly edition, the *Weekly Herald* (later the *Yeoman)* with considerable success. As time went on he also became more and more involved in the affairs of the town and he was known as a man who was forthright in his views. His friends also got to see another side of the Ulster exile and spoke of his soft-hearted and kindly personality. He also earned friends through his involvement in social and community life, helping to found the Wanganui and Rangitikei Land and Building Society and the local Oddfellows Lodge and a chess club. In March 1868, however, Fanny Ballance died after a short illness, at the age of just 24. Two years later, at Wellington, on 19 May 1870, John Ballance married Ellen Anderson, the daughter of Wellington merchant David Anderson. There were no children from either marriage, but in 1886 Ellen and John adopted Ellen's four-year-old niece, Florence Anderson, whom they re-christened Kathleen.

Ballance's entry into politics was not exactly a smooth one; in 1872 he put his name forward at a parliamentary by-election, but withdrew before the vote. Three years later he narrowly won in another constituency, but increased his majority at the general election of 1876. His rise to prominence had begun and would continue with his appointment in January 1878 as Commissioner of Customs, Commissioner of Stamp Duties and Minister of Education for the Gray government. Shortly afterwards he became Colonial Treasurer – high office for a relatively young and politically inexperienced man, but he resigned in 1879 after quarrelling with the authoritarian Grey. In 1884 he would return to government office, being appointed to the lands and immigration, native affairs and defence portfolios. Through his Land Act of 1885, which was a major piece of legislation, he sought to place as many people as possible on the land by encouraging leasehold tenure and establishing government-assisted special settlement schemes. As native minister he carried forward a policy aimed at protecting Maori land from private sale. Ballance also visited Maori throughout the North Island and made an effort to acquire some proficiency in their language.[303] In due course, John Ballance would achieve much more and would indeed become Prime Minister of New Zealand, one of two Ulstermen who rose to prominence in this way. His ancestral home at Glenavy is now open to the public.

In Limavady there is a statue in honour of the second of the New Zealand Prime ministers with the strongest of Ulster links, William Ferguson Massey. Born in Limavady and educated in Londonderry, he emigrated in 1870 to join his parents, who had gone with a group of Nonconformist emigrants in 1862, and over 50 years later would return to his native province as Prime Minister of New Zealand. The visit in November 1923 saw Massey feted in Belfast, but the warmest welcome awaited him in his old home

town. In the city, Belfast Chamber of Commerce hosted a luncheon for the Prime Minister, during which the President, Sir WF Coates said that "Mr Massey was a son of Ulster, of whom Ulster was justly proud".[304] Massey, who had arrived in Belfast the previous morning on the Liverpool steamer, noted that there were many Ulstermen and sons of Ulstermen in the New Zealand parliament and government, and, he said, the two countries were very similar in their characteristics ". . . and activated by the same patriotic spirit of loyalty to the Crown and love and admiration for the Empire which their ancestors built up."

When he went to Queen's University to receive an honorary degree of Doctor of Laws, a Maori welcome had been prepared on the lawns by the students, while the next day Massey visited Londonderry and Limavady. In the latter town a guard of honour of Royal Ulster Constabulary welcomed him to the Memorial Institute where among the guests at an evening reception were many old school friends.

William Ferguson Massey, who was born in Limavady, County Londonderry, and became Prime Minister of New Zealand.

The next day the New Zealand Premier's thoughts must have focused on his childhood, as he attended a service at Second Limavady Presbyterian Church, where he had worshipped as a boy. That afternoon, reports inform us, he watched a church parade by members of the 'B' Special Constabulary before enjoying a luncheon presented in his honour by the ladies of the Limavady district.[305]

"The foundations of Mr Massey's career were laid in Ulster" the *Northern Whig* newspaper of 29 November proudly declared, outlining that in 1894, at the age of 38, he had been elected a member of the New Zealand parliament, rising within the ranks of the opposition Reform Party and becoming its leader in 1903. He became the New Zealand Prime Minister in 1912, having served as Minister of Lands, Agriculture and Labour, Industry and Commerce previously. He was, said the *Northern Whig*, a politician who had steered New Zealand through the post-war depression and who was " . . . a big, kind, natural, unassuming man."

"In his life story we see the triumph of character, and though we claim to be a modest people we are not a little proud of his success. We find the secret in the records of County Londonderry and of Limavady", the paper said.[306]

During his visit Massey, who died in 1925, reminded those who attended a lunch at the Ulster Reform Club in Belfast's Royal Avenue, that there had been so many emigrants from the north of Ireland to North Island in New Zealand, that it had been referred to as 'Ulster'. The trip was his fifth and last visit to Britain. He was unwell and returned to New Zealand ill and tired on 24 January 1924. Cancer progressively weakened him and by October he was forced to relinquish many of his duties as Prime Minister. An operation in March 1925 was unsuccessful and on 9 April he returned from hospital to his home, where he died on 10 May 1925 at the age of 69 years. He was buried at Point Halswell at the entrance to Wellington Harbour, where, in September 1930, a large memorial was unveiled.

Another New Zealand political with local connections was Peter Butler, who emigrated following the end of the First World War and became prominent in the labour and trade union movement. In the post-Second World War era he was a close friend of the New Zealand Premier, Peter Fraser, who, while on an official visit to Northern Ireland in 1948, took time to visit Carrickfergus, home of Butler's 91 year-old mother.[307]

Prominent Canadian politician Alexander McNeill named his home 'Corran', after his birthplace at Larne on the Antrim Coast, and was, like Massey, a proud Imperialist and Empire Loyalist. McNeill was born at Larne in 1842, the son of a prominent landed family with strong connections to Scotland. He was educated in England and at Trinity College in Dublin before embarking on a career as a lawyer. In 1872, newly married, he and his wife, who was also his second cousin, Hester Law Howard, emigrated to Canada and settled on a 300-acre farm near the town of Paisley. A few years later he would purchase another farm on the Bruce peninsula, near the town of Wiarton, and would name his home there after the one he had left behind on the Antrim coast.

When McNeill entered politics he would be known for his conservative and imperialist views, and he became Member of Parliament for Bruce North in the Canadian House of Commons in 1882, serving until 1901. In addition to his parliamentary duties for his constituency, McNeill became a national figure in Canada noted for his uncompromising views on ties to Britain remaining strong, and he was for a time vice president of the Imperial Federation League, which promoted links to the 'Mother Country' in opposition to others, such as French Canadians, who held somewhat different views. McNeill has been described by his biographer as "a fascinating historical character who made a distinctive contribution to his region and played a role in national events". Yet McNeill's story is not without pathos. His wife died in 1890 at a young age, leaving her politician husband to raise their son Malcolm, something which was problematical given his father's frequent political journeys across Canada. McNeill brought servant girls from Ireland (probably from Larne) over to his house, and his own personal gardener, a man called James Eyre, maintaining something of a connection with home. But the Corran is today a ruined edifice, forming part of a park area; McNeill died in 1932 at the age of 90, Malcolm never married and the estate dwindled with the passing years. The last of the McNeills of the Bruce Peninsula died in 1956, the Corran itself was to become a sad memorial to their passing.[308] (see picture on page 102.)

There have been many Ulster emigrants who have played a political role in the lands of their adoption. Few would have such a pivotal part to play as the orphan emigrant Charles Thomson, one of six children who lost their father, when he died on the ship taking the family from their native County Londonderry in 1739. Thomson began his new life as an indentured servant in Philadelphia, but would rise to prominence as the Secretary to the Continental Congress during the Revolutionary War, and the man who drafted out the American Declaration of Independence in his own hand.[309] Strabane man John Dunlap later printed it.

Another man with Strabane connections later rose to prominence for the United States as an ambassador to Russia during the Cold War period. Admiral Alan G Kirk was appointed to the position in 1949 and was a nephew of Mrs Sinclair, Holyhill, Strabane, paying visits to her several times during the Second World War. In 1938 he was Naval Attaché to the US embassy in London and was in charge of American forces at the Sicily and Normandy landings. When victory celebrations were held at the end of the war, Kirk rode in the second car in the New York Victory parade, directly behind General Eisenhower.[310]

The ruins of The Corran, Wiarton, on Ontario's Bruce peninsula. Once the home of the McNeill family, they named it after their home at Larne in County Antrim. Alexander McNeill was a member of the Canadian Parliament for Bruce North, Ontario, between 1882 and 1901.

courtesy A Burke, Ontario

British North America afforded opportunity for many to play a prominent political part in their communities, one of many being William Robinson, a County Antrim emigrant to Ontario and twice Mayor of Kingston, a city known as the 'Derry of Canada' because it had so many Ulster emigrants. In addition to his part in city politics and government, William Robinson was also a Member of Parliament, being elected firstly as an Independent in 1870. A Presbyterian, and an Orangeman, he died in his 88th year in 1912, and was said to have been one of the most prominent men in Kingston municipal matters for over 40 years – an impressive tribute indeed.[311]

Ulster emigrants played important roles in other parts of the world as well. For example, in 1900 Robert Hugh Henderson of Kimberley, South Africa, was far removed from his native County Armagh. His father, James Henderson, was a farmer at Kildarton near the city. Henderson was Mayor of Kimberley in 1900 and would also become a South African Member of Parliament[312] In Australia there were also many to be found in the political arena. A County Antrim father and son served on the council in the Charters Towers district of North Queensland, for example. John Gordon Verner had been an alderman in the Hughenden area, while his son Samuel J Verner, was Mayor of Charters Towers when the town was visited by the then Prince of Wales. The

Robert Hugh Henderson of Kildarton, County Armagh, who became a Member of Parliament in South Africa.

family was from Islandmagee.[313] In 1913 William Davison was another Ulster exile who was a Mayor – in his case the Royal Borough of Kensington. A County Antrim man who had many connections with Ballymena and Whiteabbey, he was a barrister and Freeman of the City of London and had also apparently been one of the first in the city to sign the Ulster Covenant protesting against Home Rule for Ireland, in September 1912.[314]

There are countless many other examples of such participation in civic life by Ulster people far from their homeland. These examples continue through the years; in 1974, for example, Robert G Logan of Larne was appointed

THE HON. W.H. IRVINE
– PREMIER OF VICTORIA.

In the early years of the 20th century the premier of Victoria, Australia, was WH Irvine of Newry, County Down. His father was Hill Irvine of Dromalane Mill in the town and the family emigrated shortly after his death. Irvine was related to John Mitchel, prominent Irish political figure in the 19th century. This sketch appeared in the *Weekly Telegraph* in 1903.

British Consul in Hong Kong. Among those with whom the Queen's University graduate was acquainted in the colony was Ulster journalist Robin Parke, then working as Sports Editor with the *South China Morning Post*.[315]

By far the most famous of those who made a name for themselves in the political field, of course, were the men who became US Presidents. The list of them, as is well-known, includes James Buchanan, Ulysses Simpson Grant, Andrew Johnson, Chester Alan Arthur, Theodore Roosevelt, William McKinley, James Polk Knox and Woodrow Wilson. Claims of Scotch-Irish ancestry were also made for Warren Harding, who died in office in 1923, and the roll of honour is obviously a lengthy one, especially when compared to those of other cultural groups. One of the foremost, and the first Ulster-Scot to enter the White House was Andrew Jackson, the son of County Antrim emigrants who had settled in the Waxhaws region of the Carolinas. He is regarded as the founder of the modern Democratic Party in the USA and enjoyed a military and political career which showed signs of tenacity and of little mercy to his opponents.[316] Jackson, who became the seventh president, was born on 15 March 1767, a short time after his father had died. Although he exhibited a wild independence, his mother Elizabeth's influence gave him a strong religious faith and respect for women. Andrew Jackson lost his mother and two brothers in the Revolutionary War, all having identified themselves with the American cause, and he himself fought on the Revolutionary side, being imprisoned at one point. Jackson also famously refused to blacken the boots of a British officer billeted in the family home, something which his brother also refused to do, and both were struck with a sword, a blow which was said to have contributed to his brother Robert's death.[317]

In the aftermath of the Revolutionary War, he moved to Salisbury, North Carolina, to commence a legal career, and was called to the Bar in 1787, becoming Attorney General of the Western District of Tennessee in 1791, the same year in which he married Rachel Donelson, something which would later cause controversy and embarrassment because it transpired that there had been an error and Rachel had not been actually divorced at the time. Jackson would have this issue return to haunt him – although not particularly harm him – when he entered election contests. His first entry into politics, however, was when he was elected in 1795 to the Constitutional Convention which drafted a constitution for Tennessee, the state he subsequently represented in the House of Representatives between 1796 and 1798. A judge in the Tennessee Superior Court between 1798 and 1804, he retired that year to concentrate on his business interests at his Hermitage plantation near Nashville.

Andrew Jackson was also emerging as a relentless Indian fighter, and his prowess as a military commander was to come before a much wider stage in January 1815 when, during war

Centrepiece at the Andrew Jackson State Park on the boundaries of North and South Carolina is this impressive statue of the young Jackson on horseback.

with Britain, he led American forces to victory at the Battle of New Orleans, later immortalised in popular song. His triumphant return to Tennessee made clear that Jackson was destined for greater things; in 1824 he was narrowly defeated in the Presidential election, but in 1828 he defeated President Adams in what was seen as a great victory for the common man.

Jackson was not a perfect figure by any means; his ruthless actions against the Indian Nations leave him open to much criticism from later historians of American history, and he also dominated his cabinet and brooked little opposition, falling out with his Vice President, fellow Ulster-Scot Carolinian John Caldwell Calhoun, who resigned from the cabinet in 1832. One reason for their lack of understanding with each other was over the issue of 'states rights', when Calhoun argued that each state had the right to secede from the Union if it wished and Jackson responded by threatening military action against any state which dared to try. The so-called Nullification Crisis which took place during Jackson's term as President was a forerunner of events to come in the

1860s when the issue would only be settled by open war.

The Hermitage in Nashville remains as a lasting memorial to the first Ulster-Scot President to enter the White House; it is where his beloved wife Rachel and he are both buried, and where thousands of visitors come each year to have recounted something of the extraordinary history of the son of County Antrim emigrants.

Like Andrew Jackson, many other Ulster-Scots emigrants and their descendants would be proud Americans, although not all would have the same combined sense of loss and value in freedom which Jackson would express. He noted in a letter in 1813 how he had lost "every thing that was dear to me" during the American Revolution and added that to maintain "the independent rights of our nation is a duty I have ever owed to my country to myself and to posterity, and when I do all I can to it support, I have only done my duty."[318] It would be a credo and love of nation which many of the Ulster-Americans would uphold through generations.

The graves of Andrew Jackson and his beloved wife Rachel at the Hermitage in Nashville. Photo by James George, County Antrim exile living in the Tennessee city.

Ulster-Scots heroes; President Andrew Jackson and General Sam Houston, both descendants of County Antrim families, feature on this First Day Cover issued by the US postal service in 1964. Houston in Texas is named after Sam Houston, whose ancestors were from Ballyboley, County Antrim.

105

[286] See Drs D Hume and JW Nelson, *The Templecorran Project*, Larne, 1994

[287] Richard Robert Madden, *The United Irishmen, Their Lives and Times, New York, Volume II*, undated; Dr D Hume, 'The Story of John Neilson c.1770–1827', *Broadisland Journal* Vol 5, 1999

[288] This information comes from K Edward Lay, *The Architecture of Jefferson County, Charlottesville and Albemarle County, Virginia*, University Press of Virginia, 2000, and K. Edward Lay, 'Jefferson's Master Builders', *UVA Alumni News*, October 1991

[289] The driving force behind erection of this monument was Kevin Donleavy of Ivy, Virginia, who provided many of the details on John Neilson in Virginia

[290] *Belfast News Letter*, 23 April 1833

[291] Lay, 'Jefferson's Master Builders', pps 18–19

[292] Kevin Donleavy, 'Dedication to the Monument of John Neilson', Maplewood Cemetery, Charlottesville, Virginia, 17 April 1999

[293] *Appletons Cyclopaedia of American Biography*

[294] ibid.

[295] *Belfast News Letter*, 2 December 1828

[296] a lasting reminder of this County Down connection with the Congress of Vienna is the presence of the chairs from the Congress at the home of Lord Castlereagh, Mount Stewart near Greyabbey, which is now in the care of the National Trust

[297] *Belfast News Letter*, 26 January 1853

[298] Donald Harman Akenson and WH Crawford, *Local Poets and Social History: James Orr, Bard of Ballycarry*, Belfast, 1977, p102–104

[299] Letter from John Nevin, 10 April 1804, Public Record Office of Northern Ireland

[300] William C Davis, *The Battle of New Market*, 1975, gives a detailed account of the engagement

[301] Margaret Wilson (18) was drowned at the stake in the Solway Firth for being a Covenanter. Family members later emigrated to the north of Ireland and eventually to America

[302] Ronnie Hanna, *Woodrow Wilson, A Presbyterian President*, Lurgan, County Armagh, 1992

[303] McIvor, Tim. 'Ballance, John 1839–1893'. *Dictionary of New Zealand Biography*, updated 11 December 2002 URL: http://www.dnzb.govt.nz/

[304] *Northern Whig*, 30 November 1923

[305] ibid., 3 December 1923

[306] *Northern Whig*, 29 November 1923

[307] *Larne Times*, 30 December 1948

[308] Allan Bartley in his book, *Alexander McNeill: A Political Life*, Bruce County Historical Society, Ontario, 1990, provides an excellent account of the County Antrim exile.

[309] Richard Hofstadter, *America at 1750. A Social Portrait*, London, 1971, p63

[310] *Weekly Telegraph*, 5 May 1949

[311] *Larne Times* and *Weekly Telegraph*, 17 August 1912

[312] *Weekly Telegraph*, 6 January 1900; *RH Henderson, An Ulsterman in Africa*, Cape Town, 1944

[313] *Larne Times*, 17 July 1920; 12 November 1921

[314] *Larne Times* and *Weekly Telegraph*, 29 November 1913

[315] *East Antrim Times*, 11 October 1974

[316] For an excellent and superbly detailed study of Jackson's life see Robert V Remini's three volume series *Andrew Jackson*, New York, 1998

[317] Remini, p21

[318] Andrew Jackson to Willie Blount, 4 January 1815, quoted in Remini, op cit

Chapter 11

Late arrival: Ulster emigrants in the 20th century

A postcard from the Great Dominion; this was sent to Donoughmore, Newry, in 1909 from Toronto, where the writer was having a holiday to mark Thanksgiving. Many thousands of Ulster emigrants found a new home in Canada.

There was an especially poignant scene at the funeral of Ulster exile Lily Conly in Winnipeg in 1950, when the pallbearers took her coffin. Formerly a prominent member of Gardenmore Presbyterian congregation in Larne, she had lived at that town's harbour district before emigrating with her husband to Canada. The pall bearers who carried her on her final journey were Harry Guest, William Marcus, John Turk, John Mathieson, James Morrow and Alex McMullan, all of them from the rural district of Drumcrow, home of her husband Andrew. It was reported in the local newspaper

that the funeral had been the occasion for a gathering of a large number of former residents of Larne and Drumcrow, evidence that a small but close-knit exile community was in existence in Winnipeg and district at the time.[319]

The significance of their native land to such people can be a very great one. During a short stay in the United States some years ago, when I was visiting schools and seeking to further twinning prospects for a local authority, I was amazed to receive a phone call at the home of my hosts from a Larne exile then living in North Carolina. Archie Craig had seen

107

Larne men Denis and Alf Whiteside and Robert McKee with members of the 25th Toronto Boys Brigade Company which they formed in Chalmers United Church. Denis had been a Staff Sergeant with the local BB company in his home town.

Denis Whiteside collection

publicity about my visit in a local newspaper and managed to track me down. He explained that he was a 'Factory man' – born in Larne's Newington Avenue district – and a former foreman in the Larne Weaving Company. Archie had moved around quite a lot, working with an airline company prior to the Second World War, spending some years in Baltimore in the United States and Montreal in Canada, marrying and settling down in the former. He had ended up near the North Carolina town of Gaffney, and his last visit home to Larne had been about 15 or 20 years before, he explained in his call. For Archie, young days remembered brought back many recollections of those he had grown up with in 'the Factory'. Born in 1913, he was 80 years old at the time and I regretted that time did not permit me to meet him. His example was a pertinent one; Archie Craig was one of the many more modern exiles who had left our shores.

The fascinating story of how Ulster exiles who were members of the Boys Brigade at home helped establish a company in Toronto comes from Denis Whiteside, now living in Brampton, Ontario. In 1949 Denis, and his brother Alf, and another exile, Bob McKee, started the 25th Toronto Company in Chalmers United Church, Mount Dennis district. The Larne man had written a weekly BB column for the *Larne Times* and was able to fulfil the same role in his new home, the publicity in the *Mount Dennis News Weekly* greatly assisting the fortunes of the new company.[320]

The role which the BB played as a familiar anchor (to use the Boys Brigade symbol as an analogy) was important to Denis Whiteside, for he had been a staff sergeant in his local BB Company. The decision to emigrate to Canada had been one which saw him leave Larne after emotional good-byes – one of his neighbours from Priory Place in the town, Anna Moore, even travelled to Belfast docks to say goodbye to him. The emigrant caught the train to Belfast, the tram to the docks and then the steamer to Glasgow, where he would spend some days at the home of an aunt in Govan, saying farewells to the Scottish branch of his family. Recalling the journey, which lasted a week on an ocean liner, he relates that his cabin companion was a father of two children and that this eased some of his concerns about seeking a new life in Canada:

> It seemed to me that he was taking a much bigger risk than I was, as he left behind a wife and family to explore a future in an unknown land far away from home.[321]

The trip, he recalls, ended up like being 'the vacation trip of a lifetime', with ample meals and snacks on the liner, and varied entertainment and activities. Whiteside was one of many anxious British immigrants to Canada who arrived at Halifax, Nova Scotia, to be greeted by friendly Customs and Immigration staff. Following clearance of Customs a long overland train journey to Toronto awaited, in the company of his cabin mate:

> The one thing that surprised us and impressed us most of all was the immense distances between towns and cities. Travelling from Larne to Belfast in under an hour seemed like nothing compared with this trip across the land from Halifax to Toronto. It was also very enlightening to experience the severity of the winter climate, compared with what we had left back home in Northern Ireland.

The presence of family members in Canada had spurred the emigration for the Larne man, and there was a warm welcome from his aunt Janet (his mother's sister) and Uncle Alf when he arrived in Union Station at Toronto. At home in Larne the Whitesides did not have a car, and the first indications of a different lifestyle across the Atlantic came through the fact that his aunt and uncle had driven from Willowdale outside Toronto to meet up with him; they were the first relatives of his to have ever been able to afford a car. Aunt Janet had become a benefactor, encouraging him to come to Canada and even buying the tickets for his journey. Many years later Denis recalled:

> The car trip up Yonge Street in Toronto to Hillcrest Avenue in Willowdale was a real eye-opener to me, and from the multiple high-rise skyscrapers to the beautiful landscaped parks, and the modern bungalow type homes in well-laid out sub-divisions, it immediately became clear to me that I was going to enjoy my time in Canada.

Although his aunt and uncle were comfortably off, it was clear that family sacrifices were being made to accommodate him; the dining room in their home had been converted into a bedroom, with a pull out Chesterfield bed which had to be folded up when the dining room was needed. Denis was fortunate in having two cousins, Mary and Margaret, who helped him integrate into his new society by introducing him to friends and acquaintances, taking him to the movies and the local church. A socialisation process soon got underway and was followed by a search for job opportunities. The latter took some time, however, but one day when Denis arrived at the Fruehauf Trailer Company of Canada for an interview for a draughtsman's position he had the good fortune to find

Denis Whiteside swapped a house at Mill Road in Larne for this one in Hillcrest Avenue, Willowdale, Toronto.   *Denis Whiteside*

that another Irish exile, a man called Jimmy Crichton, was hiring for the drawing office of the firm. Finding that Denis was from Northern Ireland, he was hired for his first job. There were some immediate differences from his old job as a draughtsman in James Mackie & Sons in Belfast, but they were minor:

> On my drawings I was not allowed to spell the word tyre as tyre, but was made to change it to tire, similarly the word colour had to be color with no U, and also I was now a draftsman and not a draughtsman.

The family network would, within a short time, assist in bringing his brother Alf and his mother to Canada, the family roots in Larne being lifted. Initially the family stayed with Janet and Alf in Willowdale, but accommodation was, not surprisingly, cramped, and the search for a house ended at Mount Dennis, where the Whitesides would begin the process of integration through socialisation with those around them and involvement in the local church and the Boys Brigade. It would be a familiar emigrant story, with variants depending on the emigrants.

Although Denis Whiteside would meet his wife-to-be in Canada, there was a distinct band of emigrants from Ulster in the 20th century that had met their husbands after they had crossed the Atlantic in the other direction. The GI Brides were an important although small group of emigrants from the province in the 1940s, their departure producing modern links, particularly with the United States.

Among those who were GI brides was Margaret Burton of Irish Quarter West, Carrickfergus, who entered the history books in her native town by being the first GI bride to leave. She had married Lieutenant Ivor W McKay of Lakeland, Florida, at St Nicholas Church in the town two days before Christmas 1944.[322] Eileen Adams of Larne was among the girls who married Canadians. She married a major in the army and lived at Regina, Saskatchewan, until 1948 when her husband was discharged and joined the Diplomatic Service, being posted to Northern Canada as government representative to the Innuit Nation, and later to Ottawa. The couple had five sons; Patrick, who also became a diplomat, John, a geologist, Kevin, a transport manager, Kenny, a radio technologist, and Michael, who worked with the Peace Corps in Mozambique. The family included two brothers in Larne (Mervyn and Frank), another brother in Canada (John) and William, who made a new life in New Zealand, showing how geographically spread Ulster families could become.[323]

Another GI Bride was Beatrice Seay of Portadown, who had settled in Cincinnati and had a two-year old daughter by April 1949. She wrote home to Ulster to debunk suggestions in a magazine that most GI brides were unhappy and isolated in their new homes.[324] The former Portadown woman lived, appropriately enough for an Ulster exile, in Colerain Avenue, Cincinnati, and wrote that she loved America:

> . . . and have found many friends over here who have gone out of their way to make me feel thoroughly at home. Sure, I feel homesick at times to see Mom, Dad, brother and sister at 189 West Street, Portadown. We all do, and we wouldn't be very good daughters if we didn't, but I wouldn't change my husband or the life I lead for all the money in the USA.

Mary May Montgomery of Mossley married at Crawfordsville, Indiana, in 1946, the aisle of the Methodist Church being strewn with petals. The isolation of the GI bride comes across in the account of her wedding, for few members of her family appear to have been able to travel across the Atlantic for the occasion, and the bride was given away by the groom's brother. Home was not forgotten though, since a recording of the wedding ceremony was made and sent back home to County Antrim.[325]

Although there were many GI brides, few can have poems written about their departure, as was the case with Ruby Mewhirter, daughter of a railway guard in County Antrim. The train station where she worked was also the place of employ of John MacNeill, a native of County Tyrone known in Ballycarry village as 'the Porter Poet'. A special presentation of a leather writing folder was made to Ruby at Ballycarry railway station to mark her departure for a new life in Baltimore in January 1946.[326] The daughter of Guard Sam Mewhirter of Meeting-house Street, Larne, she had married an American GI soldier and was bound for Baltimore to join her husband. John MacNeill would be inspired to write *Ballycarry's Farewell to a GI Bride*:

> Dear Ruby, now you've gone away,
> How grim and dreary hangs the day
> Our hearts that once were light and gay
> are sunk and low,
> Since that dark hour we heard you say
> 'Twas time to go.

> I realise, ah, woe betide,
> The fact that you're a GI bride,
> And that you're for the other side
> To join the Yanks
> Who've gathered up our country's pride
> With de'il the thanks.

> There's things we could much better spare
> Than Irish colleens, dainty, fair,
> Whose humour, wit and gracious air
> Have long been famed
> And held in honour everywhere
> Where woman's named.

> We gave to them in days of yore
> Eleven Presidents or more,
> Some gallant generals, half a score,
> From Erin's Isle,
> Who placed their colours at the fore
> In Irish style.

> But what's the use to say them nay
> In present, as in bygone days,
> A lad and lass will have their way
> When love comes in;
> Once cupid enters on the fray
> He's sure to win.

> Since this is so, we wish you joy,
> The usual girl and then the boy,
> And happiness and lasting joy
> Through married life –
> One thing that money cannot buy
> For man or wife.

> God speed you safely o'er the foam
> To Liberty's empanelled dome:
> No matter where your feet may roam,
> Or may they tarry,
> The best of luck from all at home
> In Ballycarry.[327]

Her wartime romance started with a GI named Charles Rudzinski, whom she was introduced to by a soldier who had met her at the local Methodist Church. When she met Charles again it was at a dance in a local ballroom, the Pavilion. Her best friend also met up with a GI, and both would marry the young men and make a new life in the USA. Ruby recalled how Cameron Ramsey's band struck up *Who's taking you home tonight* and her GI asked "Who is taking you home tonight?" The Larne girl replied "I guess you are" and the romance was born.

Her father had discouraged against his daughter dating Americans, so when the GI arrived at the door one evening there was a dilemma for Ruby, resolved when her mother told her to invite Charles into the house:

Daddy was shining his shoes for work at the railway and I said I had an American in the parlour and called Charles to come in, and introduced them. Daddy loved to talk and so the conversation went on and on. When Charles left Daddy said that he seemed to be a nice young man and so the romance continued.

Ruby recalls:

Peggy (her best friend) and Frank started dating and of course we double dated a lot and enjoyed being together. We'd also go for walks sometimes up the Ballymena line to the beetling engines, we'd lean over the stone wall overlooking the stream there and as Frank sang exactly like Bing Crosby we'd all sing "You are my sunshine". Islandmagee was another favourite place, we'd go over on the ferry and walk to the golf course, it was lovely there. We rode bicycles too; our entertainment was a simple life style, but we always had fun.

Charles and I started walking out along the Coast Road and stopped at the Devil's Churn[328], we went down the steps to see the water swirling all around and that's where I got my first kiss – isn't that romantic?

Ruby worked at the office of the railway goods depot in Larne, her American boyfriend at the depot itself and she would often find that he had left candy and oranges in her bicycle bag; a treat when everything at home was rationed.

Ruby relates from her home in Baltimore:

We were together most every day and he came to my house a lot – by this time our romance was getting serious. All in my family were really fond of Charles and spoke so highly of him. My family seemed to accept the fact that we would marry and were pleased. In May of 1944 we became engaged and my Auntie Gretta gave us an engagement party; it was a very exciting time for us. We dated about two years. Charles and Frank were moved to Moneymore and came every weekend to Larne.

On the men's way back to camp on Sunday nights Ruby and her friend, Peggy Greenlees, would travel by train to Belfast with them and walk along York Street, where the GIs caught a bus. She remembers:

We'd kiss good-bye then start walking back, turning to wave a lot and they did too until they were out of sight. When I think of it, it makes me laugh.

In due course the wedding was planned for Larne Methodist Church on 28 September 1944. The wedding gown and veil were sent from the United States by Charles Rudzinski's sisters and gifts soon began pouring into the Mewhirter home. Charles, who had been posted to England, came back the day before the wedding, and on the day itself Ruby says she was "floating on a cloud". There were many outside the church and not a spare seat available inside. Afterwards a reception at the family home was followed by a honeymoon in Portrush for a few days, then Ruby's GI was

GI bride Ruby Mewhirter and her husband Charles Rudzinski on their wedding day at Larne Methodist Church on 28 September 1944.
courtesy Ruby Rudzinski, Essex, Baltimore

back to his camp in southern England. In May 1945 they would meet up again, when they spent a week in Stratford-on-Avon, and it would be their last time together before Charles went back home to the United States.

On the couple's first wedding anniversary Charles arrived back in New York, on board the *Queen Mary*, and the Andrews Sisters were there to welcome the returning soldiers, singing "I'll be with you in apple blossom time". His Larne bride would later reflect how appropriate that was, since she arrived in New York the following spring.

The day she left Larne was, not surprisingly, a very sad one. Her parents and sister and other relatives went to Belfast to see Ruby leave for America. When the train passed Ballycarry station noisemakers were detonated on the rails as a farewell, and she recalls how touching she found that. She was among the Ulster women who sailed out from Belfast on the SS *Henry Gibbons* on 3 April 1946. Ruby remembers:

Being far away from home was made easier for GI bride Ruby Mewhirter through the welcome she received from her husband's family.
courtesy Ruby Rudzinski

An advertisement from the *Larne Times* of June 1946 aimed at encouraging GI brides to subscribe to the newspaper.

The water was calm but when we got way out in the Atlantic the waves were tremendous – I couldn't believe it. I was seasick for three days. I couldn't wait to get on dry land after seven days. After sighting the Statue of Liberty I watched it all day, it was an impressive sight; the boat seemed to be going very slowly now.

Our boat docked (I guess it was in Manhattan) towards evening and the lights in New York made it look like fairy land....Meeting Charles again was like a dream. We spent the weekend in the city, which was wonderful. We went to Radio City Music Hall, where the Rockettes dancers always perform. The big name orchestra on stage was Xaviaer Congat with his Latin orchestra – I was mesmerized. Charles bought me an orchid.

Imagine all this happening to a wee girl from Larne . . .

On the train journey to Baltimore, Ruby's concern was how her husband's family would accept her. She need have had no concerns. One sister had a holiday home about an hour from Baltimore and took the couple there for a week to relax. The family even had a 'Welcome Home' sign made to welcome them, and after they had moved to their home Charles's two sisters visited every day for six months, showing Ruby around Baltimore while Charles worked at the Western Electric Company in the city.

You had to wait five years to become a citizen, and 12 February 1952 (Lincoln's Birthday) was an exciting day for Ruby; she officially became a US citizen. It was many years later, however, when the local baseball team was having a parade through the area and she found herself joining as enthusiastically in the cheering as everyone else that she realized she truly was an American.

Ruby and Charles Rudzinski on their 50th wedding anniversary in 1994.

welcomed them all as did Charles. For me it was a breath of home, especially as they were all from Larne.

Ruby wrote home to Larne each week and kept in close contact with all her friends; at Christmas for many years she was sending an average of 200 Christmas cards back across the Atlantic.

Four of her friends from Larne were also GI brides – Peggy Greenlees and Peggy Morris lived in Chicago, her cousin Ellie Mewhirter lived at Rochester in New York, and Betty Cochrane ended up in Kentucky. Other Larne women she knew married GIs and came to the states included Marjorie Bell, Molly Wallace, Iris Johnson, and Maureen McLaughlin. Her best friend Peggy and husband Frank would return to Baltimore for a special occasion in 1994, when Ruby and her sweetheart Charles celebrated fifty years of being happily married. They also brought with them an etching of Larne Methodist Church, where it had all begun in 1944. Charles Rudzinski passed away four years later, leaving his Larne-born wife with many happy memories.[329]

Links with the GI brides continued through the mail that passed between the exiled daughters and those at home, but in some areas contact was more formalised. In Larne, for example, a GI Association was set up to maintain links between those such as Ruby Mewhirter who had married Americans and also their families at home. One social function of the Association took place in 1949 to mark the departure of one Mrs Roddy, who was leaving the town for six months to stay with her daughter and son-in-law in Ohio.[330] Some time later there was an Overseas Association in the town, which may have evolved from the GI Association.

Not all GI brides had wonderfully happy experiences, unfortunately. When Belfast woman Mrs Phelan of Earl Haig Crescent, was assisted to visit her daughter in California in 1948, the visit cheered up a woman who had been two years in the Bard Tuberculosis Sanatorium. Mrs John Olivares' mother had worked in a Belfast jam factory and had been assisted by colleagues there in trying to raise the money for a fare to America. Eventually she had gone to the Northern Ireland GI Bride's Parent's Association, whose financial support had made the trip possible. Her three month visit, she later told the provincial press, had done her daughter considerable good. For the Belfast GI bride, married in the city in 1945, her new life in the United States had become something of a nightmare; she had only been in her new home a short time before contacting TB and ending up in the sanatorium, proof that not all the Ulster brides had a fairy tale ending to their stories.[331]

One bride who travelled from Australia to Ulster to be married was herself the daughter of a Belfastman who had made a new home in South Australia. Arthur Johnston, an exile who lived in Port Pirie in the state, made it a point to entertain anyone from Northern Ireland who came to his

Home was not forgotten, however, for she was receiving a copy of the *Larne Times* each week, while Head Line ships from Ulster called at Baltimore to load grain. On board those ships were Larne men, who got her address from family and friends and would call during their time in the city, among them Billy Brownlees, who had worked with Ruby on the railway, Captain Billy Close, Tommy Seymour, who would later become a Mayor of Larne, and Billy Robinson. Ruby also recalls:

Herbie Houston was Captain of a ship which came to Baltimore to load cars. His sister Winnie came with him. She was a schoolteacher, a friend of mine gave her my name and she called me and we went down to see them. The ship's quarters were great. I took Winnie shopping and next day brought them to our home and took them to dinner. Herbie was good friends with my Magill cousins from 'Sunnyside' on Old Glenarm Road, Larne, so it's a small world after all. I

adopted town. One such visitor had been a young radio officer named William John Agnew, who was from Randalstown in County Antrim. He and Lillian Johnston, daughter of his host, maintained contact and in the summer of 1945 she walked down the aisle at First Antrim Presbyterian Church, having travelled some 5,000 miles to be married.[332] There were very few such instances, although exiles often made visits to their homeland or the land of their fathers. James A Preston, who was Mayor of the town of Wellington in Australia on a number of occasions, took the opportunity to return to Northern Ireland (he was a native of Banbridge) in 1949 and look in on old friends.[333] In the 1960s some Ulster people found the prospect of life in southern Africa appealing, and among them was Agnes Ferris McCurdy of Meadow Street in Larne, who returned home on a visit from Plumtree in Rhodesia in 1960.[334] The town also had a native, Paddy Shields, who was a Member of Parliament for Bulawayo.

Although not GI brides, there are accounts in many local newspapers in Ulster in the 20th century of Ulsterwomen being married in other lands. Agnes Kidd of Whiteabbey, County Antrim, was among them, and was married in 1924 at Calgary in Canada. Interestingly, she married another Whiteabbey man, James Gourley.[335] The Bishop of Singapore officiated at the wedding in 1914 of Ulster couple Captain William Moore of Ballygally, County Antrim, and Violet Moore of Londonderry and Belleek.[336] Although Roberta McConnell did not marry another Ulster exile when she was wed in Clinton, Ontario, in the 1970s, there was no mistaking a strong Ulster presence at the event; her sister Carol was one of the bridesmaids, the second being a friend named Margaret McConaghy from Craigyhill in her home town of Larne. Her parents, aunt and another friend had all travelled across the Atlantic for the occasion, bringing the bridesmaids dresses made by the bride's mother Winnie McConnell.[337]

Often it was not love but the need for employment which drove many to emigrate. Richard Robinson began his working life in the shipyard at Larne, where he started as an apprentice in 1916, then became a member of the 'A' Special Constabulary and a Prison Officer, serving on the internment ship *Argenta*, then anchored in Larne Lough. After the turbulent early years of the Northern Ireland state, Robinson signed up on an iron ore ship for a time, then on a vessel owned by the United Fruit Company of Boston, along with three other Larne men – Bill Nelson of Glynn, Tom Browne of Islandmagee and Charles O'Boyle of Larne, the latter of whom would return to Britain after a period. Richard Robinson married Larne hairdresser Marion Beattie in New York in 1946 and had an eventful life in the land of his adoption. He went to work in the Brooklyn Navy Yard and was offered a position at Pearl Harbor, Hawaii, being assigned as a junior officer on board the battleship *Utah*. The vessel was used as a target ship and her sailors went under

the armoured decks while planes dropped water bombs on her. It would not be water bombs, but the Japanese attack on Pearl Harbor which he and others would have to contend with, however, and the *Utah* did not survive the attack; "The old ship was at anchor with several other battle wagons at Battleship Row. No doubt you know the rest of the story," Robinson wrote in 1992.[338]

His subsequent career included sailing on supply runs to the Philippines and Vietnam ports during the war. Interestingly, proof of emigrant networks comes through Richard Robinson's story, for during a visit to Larne he was asked by local man Alex Ellis if he would act as sponsor to allow him to emigrate to the United States. Ellis lived for a time in Los Angeles, but later obtained a job in the *Phoenix Gazette* newspaper in Arizona. He also organised a soccer league in Phoenix[339]

Another former employee of the Larne shipyard who emigrated to North America was Thomas Smith, who arrived in Vancouver, Canada, at a much earlier time. Indeed, in 1912 he and his wife celebrated their silver wedding anniversary, with several exiles from Belfast and County Antrim being among the guests at a celebration in their Second Street North home. One of the guests was another Larne man, Andrew McNeill, accompanied by his wife.[340]

When Hugh McConnell and his wife marked their 65th wedding anniversary in Victoria, Australia, in 1946, nine children, 30 grandchildren and 22 great-grandchildren were

Richard Robinson, an Ulster exile who witnessed the Japanese attack on Pearl Harbor.

present; McConnell's wife was an Australian, but he was native of County Antrim and the last surviving member of a family of ten: He had left Larne when he was 16 years old.[341] At Winnipeg in 1942 the Glens of Antrim was strongly represented when the Wilsons of Deerpark celebrated their silver wedding, Ballymena man James Stewart acting as Master of Ceremonies, and members of the Morrow, Rea, McClure, Montgomery, Robinson, Price, Steele, Alexander, Conly, Galbraith, Marcus and Chisholm families being present.[342]

Emigration was actively encouraged by many areas, and the recommendation of someone from one's own neck of the woods was no doubt a great encouragement. Such was the case in 1924 when William Boyle Hill returned to visit his native Islandmagee, stressing to the local newspaper and a gathering of friends and former neighbours the benefits of settling under the Southern Cross. Hill was reported as saying that:

> Speaking of Australia generally, I do not say that you will pick up gold at your feet; but I do say that it offers golden opportunities for all who care to take advantage of them and in various ways. We have room for as many tradesmen as you care to send to us. Last year when we were engaged on some building operations, we advertised for men that were needed, and did not get a solitary reply. Plumbers would scarcely work for 4s an hour, and in some cases they had to be paid 6s an hour. So you can see how badly we are handicapped in the building trade for the want of proper tradesmen...The one thing I desire to impress is that there is not a man who has come to Australia from Ulster who has not made a success of it. The only man who could be said not to have made a success of it was the man who spent his money in the public house. The trouble is that we have not enough of Ulstermen in Australia. We have men from other parts of the world; but none of them has the stamina, the push, and the enterprise of the man from the North of Ireland.[343]

Hill had emigrated to Australia in 1882 and was a traveller for a firm manufacturing hardware machinery for mining operations, travelling extensively. He then entered into business on his own and was living in Sydney, New South Wales, in 1924, although he recommended would-be emigrants to consider settling in Queensland or Western Australia. In Queensland, he said, the possibilities were vast, and he extolled opportunities elsewhere; "In Western Australia, wheat, timber, and fruit also grow splendidly, and there are enormous tracts of land available for all who go out to that part of the continent . . . ", he said. It was hardly surprising that the *Weekly Telegraph* would describe Hill as ". . . a man in love with the land of his adoption" and added that ". . . he holds out the brightest prospects to those who desire to do better in life, should they emigrate to the Southern Continent."

Someone with a vested interest in encouraging Ulster emigration to Australia was William Cowzer, a Belfastman who was an Old Boy of Methodist College and was appointed Migrants Interviewing and Selection Officer to Australia House

in London in 1954. He and his wife had only been four years in Australia at the time, and was taking the opportunity while in the capital to attend the conference of Ulster Associations, he being reportedly the founder of one of these, the Ulster Association of Western Australia.[344]

The inevitable outcome of the successful encouragement to emigrate was the farewells which were held at home, the emigrants' wakes as they were descriptively known in the Glens of Antrim. Departure, although tinged with sadness, was somewhat different in the 20th century, of course, since there was the prospect of better communication between those departing and those remaining at home. There was also, in the post-1945 period, even greater prospect of the emigrants coming home to visit some years into the future, a prospect not likely in the 18th and 19th centuries for most families. This did not make the departing any less tearful for many, of course, and presentations became social occasions to say farewell in an organised fashion, as was the case in 1949 when Whiteabbey Weaving Company employees said farewell to one of their number. Agnes Boyce was bound for Australia in the summer of 1949 and a reception was provided for her in the British Legion Hall in the village, with the Works Manager making a presentation to her on behalf of her colleagues.[345]

While some emigrants would be departing as individuals or as couples, there were also instances of families on the move. In 1925, for example, James Montgomery of Glenarm was photographed on board the P&O liner *Baradine* with his wife and eleven children, the youngest just one month old, as they sailed for Australia.[346] There are numerous photographs of families bound for a new life, often showing little of the enthusiasm which must have fired them and much of the apprehension that leaving home brought for adults and children alike.

While some of the emigrants provided accounts of varying lengths of their lives at home and in their adopted homes, few managed to produce a book as did Robert Hugh Henderson of County Armagh. In *An Ulsterman in Africa* he related his early beginnings:

> I was educated at Drumbee National School. I have met boys from Drumbee in my travels in Canada and Australia. Even in South America there is a monument to another of them, which faces you as you enter the great city of Buenos Aires in Argentina. This was a certain 'Brown' who helped to relieve the Argentine from the yoke of Spain.[347]

At the age of 21 Henderson left his native county for a new life in South Africa. It was a path which others had already taken, as he recalled in his book. Two Ulstermen he had known from home introduced him to other exiles:

> I met there seven other young Ulstermen and one young lady, and for the first time since leaving Armagh, I felt really at home. These were all young men, but coming men, and though they have all passed on (I attended the funeral of the

The Montgomery family of Glenarm prepare to set sail for Australia in April 1925; James Montgomery and his wife with their eleven children, the youngest of which was one month old, on the P&O liner *Baradine*, en route to a new life in the land of the Southern Cross.

Larne Times and Weekly Telegraph, 25 April 1925

last of them in Johannesburg not so long ago), they were all men who made their mark in South Africa and each of them was a credit to the land of their adoption. The work of each and all of them is indelibly stamped on the progress of South Africa. I only give their names. There was WM Cuthbert from Belfast; John Orr from Benburb; Joseph Holdcroft from Glaslough; James Johnston from Armagh; JD Carson from Enniskillen; James Gray from Markethill; WB Morrison from near Dublin and Miss Orr from Benburb, who later became Mrs Morrison. James Johnston and James Gray met me at the boat and brought me to this little band of Ulstermen. I was an 'Ulsterman in Africa', but I felt very much at home already.[348]

The County Armagh exile would settle in Kimberley and later become a Mayor of the town, filling the office for the first time in 1899. His home was at Armagh House in the town, and he was among those who were besieged there during the South African War. Interestingly, among the heroes of the war was a Broughshane man, General Sir George White, who was hailed as 'the Saviour of Natal' at

home in County Antrim when he subsequently visited. The Henderson family, meanwhile, did not confine itself to South Africa; Robert Hugh Henderson had a brother, Tom, in the Philippines, an aunt in Ohio in the United States and a cousin called Platt who was a United States Senator.[349] During a visit to his cousin in Washington DC, Henderson was introduced to US President William McKinley, whose ancestors were from County Antrim, one of many US presidents with Ulster links. Henderson knew others in high office as well. Among them was his old friend Dick Seddon, Prime Minister of New Zealand, while a friend from school at Drumbee, Billy Ross, became a temperance reformer and a Member of Parliament in neighbouring Australia.[350] Robert Hugh Henderson would himself become a Member of Parliament in his adopted land, being elected for Boksburg in 1921, high office for a past pupil of Drumbee National School.

Interestingly at least one other of the Mayors of Kimberley was an Ulsterman. John Orr was a native of County Tyrone and had built up a considerable business in South Africa's

John Orr, County Tyrone native who was a mayor of Kimberley in South Africa on two occasions in the early 20th century.

Cape province in the drapery and outfitting trades. In 1887 he had moved to Kimberley, while his business spread from Johannesburg to Durban, Transvaal, Orange Free State, Natal, Rhodesia and elsewhere, also operating by mail order. Orr later moved his company headquarters to Kimberley, of which he was Mayor in 1910 and in 1916–18. His brother Joseph was also his business partner in South Africa, while another brother, Tom Orr, was in the boot and shoe trade in his adopted home.[351]

Not all those who intended emigrating in the 20th century actually carried it through, however. Tom Moore, a native of Ballysnod, outside Larne, was among those many hundreds who packed his bags and prepared to head off to a new future. Living in the nearby village of Millbrook in 1949 and marking his 91st birthday, he recounted in a local newspaper that on one occasion, like many other young men in the area, he had decided to emigrate to America. His bags were packed and all arrangements were made. On the day of his departure, however, just as he was about to leave the house, he related that his mother burst into tears. Moore recalled that it was too much for him; his bags were unpacked and the emigrant ship sailed with one less passenger that day.[352] It is a touching yet simple story, as touching and simple as the lives of many of the emigrants themselves.

Some years ago I wrote a story in the local newspaper about the Barry family of Magheramorne and their journey to Australia. If any reminder was needed that it is indeed a small world, it came some time later from a Scottish lady who had a copy of article sent from a relative. She in turn had sent it to a friend in Victoria, Australia, whose relatives in South Gippsland had grown up with the Barry children. The lady in question took the article to a nursing home, where Wilson Barry was living. In a letter back to Scotland, she said:

> Please thank Annie for thinking to send the paper and tell her it was a real tonic to see the interest he (Wilson) took in it. I wish you had seen his face light up when he read it.[353]

Across time, and across thousands of miles, Wilson Barry remembered his old homeland, the land he never really left.

Below; Many Ulster emigrants found pastures new across the world. This scene in the Smoky Mountains near Cherokee, North Carolina, is typical of landscapes that appealed to a rural people.

[319] *Larne Times*, 23 March 1950

[320] The author expresses thanks to Denis Whiteside of Brampton, Ontario, for sharing his memories

[321] Denis Whiteside account, unpublished memoir, Brampton, Ontario

[322] *Larne Times*, 3 January 1946

[323] Information supplied by the McKay family in Larne.

[324] *Weekly Telegraph*, 21 April 1949

[325] *Larne Times*, 4 April 1946

[326] *Larne Times*, 24 January 1946

[327] As published in the *Larne Times*, 1946

[328] The Devil's Churn is beside the Black Arch and is a sea cave where listeners can hear the waves lapping inside the rock.

[329] The author is deeply grateful to Mrs Ruby Rudzinski of Baltimore for sharing her memories as a GI bride

[330] *Larne Times*, 21 April 1949

[331] *Weekly Telegraph*, 16 December 1948

[332] *Weekly Telegraph*, 26 July 1945

[333] *Weekly Telegraph*, 4 August 1949

[334] *Larne Times*, 14 January 1960

[335] *Belfast Weekly Telegraph*, 22 March 1924

[336] *Weekly Telegraph*, 31 January 1914

[337] *East Antrim Times*, 13 September 1974

[338] Letter from Richard Robinson, Las Vegas, Nevada, 25 February 1992

[339] Newspaper clipping provided by Richard Robinson from the *Phoenix Gazette*

[340] *Larne Times*, 13 July 1912

[341] *Larne Times*, 24 January 1946

[342] *Larne Times*, 9 July 1942

[343] *Weekly Telegraph*, 12 April 1924

[344] *Weekly Telegraph*, 7 October 1954; others mentioned in the same report include JA Rutherford, an ex police officer from Londonderry who was President of the Ulster Association of Victoria; Rev James Beattie (Newtownards), Presbyterian minister at Canterbury, Victoria; Rev PJ Hayes (Bangor), a Baptist minister in Victoria; Bob Edgar (Bangor), secretary to the Mission to Lepers in Melbourne; and RG Lynn (Omagh), President of the Eastern Australia Ulster Association.

[345] *Larne Times*, 19 May 1949

[346] *Larne Times*, 25 April 1925

[347] Robert Hugh Henderson, *An Ulsterman in Africa*, Cape Town, 1944

[348] ibid., p18

[349] ibid., p89

[350] Henderson provides details in his book of meeting up with these men in later life

[351] *Belfast Weekly Telegraph*, 7 August 1926

[352] *Larne Times*, 3 February 1949

[353] Letter from MR Smith, Ayr, Scotland, 1997, in possession of the author

Bibliography

Newspapers and other publications

Belfast News Letter
Broadisland Journal, Ballycarry
East Antrim Times
Journal of Arizona History, Spring 1998
Larne Monthly Visitor
Larne Reporter
Larne Times and *Weekly Telegraph*
Northern Whig
Proceedings of the Scotch-Irish Congress of the USA
The Glynnes, Journal of the Glens of Antrim Historical Society
Ulster Folklife
Ulster Journal of Archaeology

Primary source material

Archive material from the Barry family, Australia
Delaney family, Ballycarry, County Antrim, family memoir
Henderson, RH, *An Ulsterman in Africa*, Cape Town, 1944
Irvine, Alexander, *The Souls of Poor Folk*, Belfast, 1981
Journal of John Blair, 1791, University of South Carolina, Columbia, archives
Papers of Marshall Holden, Portland, Oregon
Penny, Doug, Calgary, Alberta, memoir in the possession of the author
Public Record Office of Northern Ireland archives
Robert Witherspoon, *The Witherspoon Chronicle*, reprinted in *History of Williamsburg Presbyterian Church 1736–1981*, Kingstree, South Carolina, 1981
Robinson, Richard, Las Vegas, Nevada, memoir
Rudzinski, Ruby, Baltimore, memoirs
Semple family correspondence, Ontario, Canada
Tweed, Colin, Milton, New Zealand, information on Tweed family history
York County Historical Commission, South Carolina, archives
York District 1850 Federal Census, York, 1987
Whiteside, Denis, Brampton, Ontario, memoirs

Secondary source material

Akenson, Donald Harman and Crawford, WH, *Local Poets and Social History: James Orr, Bard of Ballycarry*, Belfast, 1997
Akenson, Donald Harman, *The Irish Diaspora*, Belfast, 1993
Alderman, Pat, *The overmountain men*, Tennessee, 1986
Appleton's Cyclopedia of American Biography
Bartley, Allan, *Alexander McNeill. A Political Life*, Ontario, 1990
Boylan, ed, *A Dictionary of Irish Biography*, Dublin, 1998
Brice, LS, The Brice family who settled in Fairfield County, South Carolina, about 1785, McCormick, South Carolina, 1956
Caldwell, Carroll S, *The Caldwell family of Spartanburg County, South Carolina*, Spartanburg, 1999
Coffey and Morgan, *Irish Families in Australia and New Zealand, 1788–1979*, Victoria, 1979
Coleman, Terry, *Passage to America*, London, 1972
Crawford and Trainor, eds, *Aspects of Irish Social History 1750–1800*, Belfast 1984

Davis, William C, *The Battle of New Market (Kentucky)*, 1975

Dennis, Gary, *The Spirit of the Twelfth*, Ontario, 1982

Dickson, RJ, *Ulster emigration to Colonial America, 1718–1775*, Belfast, 1988

Edgar, Walter, *South Carolina, A History*, University of South Carolina, Columbia, 1998

Elliott, Bruce, *Irish Migrants in the Canadas*, Kingston and Montreal, 1988

Fitzpatrick and Ickringill, eds, *Atlantic Crossroads*, Newtownards, 2001

Fitzpatrick, Rory, *God's Frontiersmen. The Scots-Irish Epic*, London, 1989

Handlin, Oscar, *Boston's Immigrants. A study in acculturation*, New York, 1974

Hanna, Ronnie, *Land of the Free, Ulster and the American Revolution*, Lurgan, 1992

Hanna, Ronnie, *Woodrow Wilson, A Presbyterian President*, Lurgan, 1992

Higginbottom, Don, *Daniel Morgan, Revolutionary Rifleman*, North Carolina, 1961

History of Indiantown Presbyterian Church, Indiantown, South Carolina, 1957

Hofstadter, Richard, *America at 1750. A Social Portrait*, London, 1971

Houston and Smyth, *The Sash Canada Wore*, Toronto, 1980

Houston and Smyth, *Irish Emigration and Canadian Settlement*, Toronto and Belfast, 1990

Hume and Nelson, *The Templecorran Project, An Historical guide to Ballycarry Old Cemetery*, Larne, 1994

James, Marquis, *The Life of Andrew Jackson*, New York, 1937

Kennedy, Billy, *Scots Irish in the Shenandoah Valley*, Belfast, 1996

Kennedy, Billy, *The Making of America, How the Scots-Irish Shaped a Nation*, Belfast, 2001

Leyburn, James G, *The Scotch-Irish. A Social History*, North Carolina, 1962

Lyle, Oscar K, Lyle Family. *The ancestry and posterity of Matthew, John, Daniel and Samuel Lyle, Pioneer settlers in Virginia*, New York, 1912

McKillop, Felix, *Glenarm. A Local History*, Belfast, 1987

McPherson, Mary-Etta, *Shopkeepers to a Nation*, Toronto, 1963

Madden, Richard Robert, *The United Irishmen. Their Lives and Times*, New York

Masonic Grand Lodge of Research Transactions, various years, Belfast and Dublin

Moss, Professor Bobby Gilmer, *The Patriots at Kings Mountain*, South Carolina, 1990

Moss, Professor Bobby Gilmer, *Journal of Capt Alexander Chesney*, South Carolina, 2002

New Zealand Dictionary of Biography

Pennefather, RS, *The Orange and the Black, Documents in the history of the Orange Order, Ontario and the West, 1890–1940*, Canada, 1984

Pettus, Louis, *The Waxhaws*, Rock Hill, South Carolina, 1993

Remini, Robert V, *Andrew Jackson (three vols)*, New York, 1998

Scotch-Irish Society of America, Proceedings of the Third Congress, Louisville, Kentucky, 1891

Scotch-Irish Society of America, Proceedings of the Sixth Congress, Des Moines, Iowa, 1894

Steen, Andrea, *Stoneboro. An Historical Sketch of a South Carolina Community*, Spartanburg, 1993

Swope, Belle McKinney Hays, *History of Middle Spring Presbyterian Church*, Pennsylvania, 1900

Trefousse, Hans L, *Andrew Johnson, A Biography*, 1991

Watson, Margaret, *Greenwood County Sketches*, Greenwood, South Carolina, 1970

Index of places mentioned in the text

Index of people mentioned in the text